New Ways for Work Coaching Manual

Personal Skills for Productive Relationships

By

Bill Eddy, LCSW, Esq. and L. Georgi DiStefano, LCSW

HIGH CONFLICT INSTITUTE PRESS
Scottsdale, Arizona

Copyright © 2015 by Bill Eddy and L. Georgi DiStefano
High Conflict Institute Press
7701 E. Indian School Rd., Ste. F
Scottsdale, AZ 85251
www.hcipress.com

Cover design by Gordan Blazevik
Book Interior design by Kristen Onesti

ORDERING MORE COPIES
Bulk rates are available on orders of 10 or more copies. Please contact HCI Press at 1-888-986-4665 or www.hcipress.com for pricing and to place orders.

ISBN: 978-1-936268-69-6
Printed in the United States of America

Negotiation and mediation expert William A. ("Bill") Eddy is president of the High Conflict Institute and a certified family law specialist. Prior to becoming a lawyer, Eddy worked as a licensed clinical social worker. He speaks throughout the U.S. and internationally about high-conflict personalities and provides consultation and training on workplace issues. He is also the author of several books on managing and responding to high-conflict people. He lives in San Diego, California.

L. Georgi DiStefano is a licensed clinical social worker with extensive experience as a therapist, Employee Assistance provider, management consultant, and a popular speaker on workplace conflict resolution. She has authored several books and articles, and has directed mental health and substance abuse programs. She lives in San Diego, California.

Bill and Georgi are coauthors of *It's All Your Fault at Work! Managing Narcissists and Other High-Conflict People* (Unhooked Books Publishing, 2015).

Learn more about the authors at www.highconflictinstitute.com.

CONTENTS

Dear Colleague,

We are very excited that you are going to be using the *New Ways for Work*™ coaching method with your clients. This is a cognitive-behavioral method which we have designed to be simple and repetitive, so that almost any employee or manager can learn these skills and apply them in their work lives – or anywhere – even during stressful times.

While this method was originally developed for employees with potentially "high-conflict" behavior in the workplace, it can be used by anyone interested in improving their interpersonal skills at work – including those who haven't had any problems and want to advance in their careers. The methods for managing one's own thinking, emotions, and behaviors will also help managers influence the thinking, emotions, and behavior of their employees in a positive manner. This method can be used with anyone.

Throughout the coaching process we emphasize a positive, "no blame - no shame" approach. We encourage you to focus on future behavior and building skills, and limit the time spent talking about feelings and the past. Employees with potentially high-conflict personalities tend to focus on the past and blaming others, but the client workbook exercises will help you focus them on the future and strengthening skills. For a more thorough explanation of our future-focused approach ("*feed forward*" we call it, rather than "feedback"), see our book *It's All Your Fault at Work! Managing Narcissists and Other High-Conflict People*.

We believe that you will enjoy working with clients using the *New Ways for Work* method, and that it will assist them in learning new skills of self-management that will please them as well.

Best wishes!

Bill Eddy, LCSW, Esq.
L. Georgi DiStefano, LCSW

INTRODUCTION TO COACHING MANUAL

The *New Ways for Work™* method provides a simple approach to learning key interpersonal skills for the workplace, structured by **The Workbook**. New "ways" simply mean new skills, which keeps the focus on the positive and learning skills for the future.

This method is designed to help clients change their own behavior. This is a different method from the CARS method we describe in our book *It's All Your Fault at Work!*, which is designed to help anyone deal with someone else's difficult behavior in the workplace. However, some clients may wish to strengthen their own self-management skills to be more effective at responding to other people's behavior, and this Workbook and method will be helpful to them as well. Many of the skills taught in the Workbook are also used with the CARS Method.

This Coaching Manual will help you guide your client through The Workbook in a step-by-step manner. It is understood that you may be an Employee Assistance Professional, a therapist who provides workplace coaching, or another form of coach – so whichever role you are in, throughout the Manual and Workbook we simply refer to you as the "Coach."

THE WORKBOOK

The Workbook is designed to be flexible for you, to use with as few as 3 coaching sessions and as many as 9 or 12 sessions. Each session includes writing exercises to help the client think through various problem situations, to practice responding to difficult situations, and to reinforce learning.

SAMPLE ANSWERS

For many of the writing exercises we have made up sample answers for your convenience, which you can share with your client or just use for your own knowledge of possible responses. Ideally, your client will answer these writing exercises first. But if he or she is having difficulty or if you want to give another example of how someone might answer, you have these samples handy. Not all questions have sample answers, as some are very specific to your client's own problems or issues.

FOR THREE SESSIONS OF COACHING

The first three sessions are self-contained. The first session gives you a chance to get acquainted, obtain your own assessment information and focus on understanding the problem or issue the client wishes to discuss. The second session introduces the four "new ways" skills: flexible thinking, managed emotions, moderate behaviors and checking yourself. The third session focuses on setting personal goals about each of these skills, for the client to remember to use in the future or to refer back to if you are going forward with more sessions.

FOR MORE SESSIONS OF COACHING

The next six sessions give more specific skills to learn within each of the four new ways skills. They include how to manage one's own emotions, write better emails, make proposals in the workplace, and generally avoid extreme behaviors. The emphasis is on keeping these skills simple and easy to remember.

If you have the opportunity to work with the client for more than nine sessions total, such as for 12 sessions, we suggest that you meet monthly to review the client's progress using the form provided titled: Continuing to Check Myself. Three copies of this form are provided, one for each follow-up session.

Of course, if you have fewer sessions, you can recommend to the client to keep and use the workbook on his or her own, filling in the practice exercises to strengthen their skills – in some cases with a review after the client has finished the workbook.

WORKSHEETS

The last section of the Workbook includes two worksheets which clients can use on their own in the future, regardless of the number of sessions you have.

HOMEWORK

While this Workbook includes some homework exercises, it is possible to have the client do all of the writing during your sessions. This gives you the ability to avoid power struggles over homework assigned and not done. Some clients will simply not do homework and there's no benefit in allowing that to become an unnecessary conflict or focus of attention.

WORKBOOK CONFIDENTIALITY

It is essential to the effectiveness of this method for the client to know from the start that this Workbook is his or her own property and intended to be totally confidential. In fact, in today's electronic world, this hand-written Workbook may be more confidential than any email or computer notes. If you have any doubts about the ability to keep this Workbook confidential, check with your professional organization about any possible exceptions. It should fit easily within the confidentiality of your role as an Employee Assistance Professional, therapist or other coaching profession.

DEALING WITH RESISTANCE

Some clients will resist using the Workbook or doing some of the exercises or taking any responsibility for their part in a problem. A simple formula for dealing with resistance is the following:

Empathize: Express empathy and respect for the client's concerns.

Educate: Explain the benefits of doing the exercises as a learning tool.

Empower: Emphasize that "it's up to you." Avoid power struggles.

FOCUS ON SKILLS FIRST

If an employee is expected to be working on stopping or changing a behavior which caused concern in the past, or wants to focus on discussing their past behavior, it is still most effective to teach the skills first and then use the skills to understand and reflect on past behavior.

DIFFICULT CLIENTS

After going through New Ways for Work, some employees may have some insight and will improve their future behavior, while others may not. Some clients referred for past negative behavior may be highly resistant or "difficult" clients. Remember, what they learn is up to them. Encourage them to practice the written and verbal exercises. If they are resistant, just educate them about their choices and the consequences of their choices, but avoid getting into a power struggle over learning and practicing these skills. If they say "No" to an exercise or want to learn something else, demonstrate your own flexible thinking by discussing what could be beneficial and demonstrate your own moderate emotions by not getting frustrated or irritated with them.

PRACTICING CONVERSATIONS

Practicing conversations with the client may be the most helpful aspect of teaching these skills. Most sessions encourage the client to discuss an issue with the coach. In these discussions, we have found it helpful to practice a future conversation in this format:

First, have the client play the part of a troubling employee or supervisor at work, while you play the part of the client. Try to demonstrate the skill that is being learned and try to give the client as many words as possible which he or she might be able to use in the future conversation.

Then, switch roles and play the part of the troubling employee or supervisor at work, while your client plays himself or herself.

Then, discuss how it felt and what the client learned from the exercise.

OTHER TOPICS

In general, the Workbook exercises can allow time for the client to talk briefly about other topics, such as family relationships or personal decisions. Ideally, you can weave these topics back into the Workbook and how they might apply the skill for the week to the situation they have raised. The client will be better off learning the skills than complaining about other people and situations. The skills will give them "new ways" of dealing with these problems, so that they won't need to feel as helpless, sad, or angry in the future about similar situations.

VENTING

If you have client who is preoccupied with the past and complaining about it, you may be tempted to just let him or her vent about it. The idea of letting them "get it off their chest" can be helpful to a majority of people. Some venting is normal and unavoidable. However, clients with maladaptive personality traits or disorders do not tend to get relief from venting and often stay stuck repeating past complaints over and over again, with intense emotions, to one person after another. If this endless cycle seems to be occurring, empathize with his or her situation and then gently focus back on the Workbook and learning the next skill. If they learn and practice the skills in the Workbook, they should have a greater ability to improve situations that frustrated them before.

FLEXIBILITY

The Workbook was based on approximately thirty years of experience dealing with clients with a wide range of workplace and legal problems. However, we offer the Workbook and Manual for your use with clients in your best judgment. These are tools for you, not rules. We encourage you to use your flexible thinking to make the best of these skills for the benefit of your clients.

FORMAT OF THIS COACHING MANUAL

Each session includes three parts:

Our coaching suggestions.

Your copy of the exact pages of the Workbook, including page numbers.

Discussion and/or sample answers to the exercises for that session.

Some of the sessions have more content than others, to allow room for more discussion. However, it is fine if you get a little behind or ahead in the Workbook.

For example, the first session is brief in terms of writing topics for your client, so that you can focus on getting acquainted. However, if you have time left over at the end of Session 1, you can go ahead and start Session 2, which has a lot of content. It may also entice your client to read ahead to get some good self-management skills right away for practical use.

The next few pages are the Introduction that your client will see in his or her Workbook.

INTRODUCTION

Jobs today are about relationships: Relationships with clients, customers, co-workers, managers, the company, and competitors. Yet the personal skills needed to manage these relationships are changing rapidly. It's common knowledge that stress from dealing with other people in the workplace is one of the largest factors affecting job dissatisfaction.

New Ways for Work: The Workbook was developed to give employees and managers training for modern work relationships while in a relationship – a coaching relationship – with an emphasis on practicing four key self-management skills: *managed emotions, flexible thinking, moderate behavior,* and *checking yourself*. Using numerous writing and discussion exercises, this workbook assists an employee or manager who wants to improve his or her workplace relationship skills while working with a coach in up to 12 coaching sessions.

IMPROVING YOUR WORKPLACE SKILLS

Some people will be learning or strengthening these four skills because they have had difficulty in a workplace relationship and were referred for this coaching to improve their skills. They may have been in "high-conflict" situations where they and/or others used the following negative behaviors:

All-or-nothing thinking (seeing oneself as perfect, others as all-bad)

Unmanaged emotions (frequent yelling, blaming, crying, dramatics)

Extreme behaviors (threats of violence, yelling, stealing, false reports, spreading rumors, etc.)

Blaming others (focusing on others' behavior; not taking responsibility for own actions)

In many high-conflict situations, only one person has these characteristics and other people are trying hard to be reasonable. In other high-conflict situations, two or more people have some of these characteristics, although one may be more extreme than the other. In order to avoid being seen as a "high-conflict person," learning and strengthening the skills in this workbook will help you do the opposite of the above behaviors.

ADVANCING IN YOUR CAREER

Others learning the skills in this workbook are doing so because they want to advance in their career. Employees and managers who wish to "move up" will benefit themselves by learning and strengthening the use of the same four self-management skills. This is because these skills help you concentrate on your goals even when facing resistance from others or other distractions. These skills will also help you assist other employees in managing difficult situations, without becoming overwhelmed yourself.

Whether you are seeking to improve your skills or advance in your career, we believe you will enjoy learning these skills and find them useful anywhere with anybody – even neighbors, friends, family, and strangers.

The 4 "New Ways" Skills are:

Flexible thinking · Managed emotions · Moderate behaviors · Checking yourself

By practicing these skills, you will be more able to: stay calm in a conflict, find solutions to problems and influence others in a positive direction.

YOUR COACH

Your coach may be an Employee Assistance Professional, a mental health professional or someone else. Throughout this workbook, we refer to your "coach," which could mean any of these roles. The main idea is that they are coaching you to strengthen your own skills rather than to solve problems for you. The type of coaching involved with this workbook is often known as "skill building." With this method, your coach will focus more on the future and less on the past, and more on what to do and less on how you feel about it. Feel free to ask questions and discuss your expectations with your coach, so that this method can be most effective for you.

A COGNITIVE-BEHAVIORAL METHOD

The method of learning contained in this book includes changing some of your thinking as well as some of your behavior. This type of approach is called a "Cognitive-Behavioral" method. This involves simple practice exercises in writing to help change some of your thinking to a more positive frame of mind. It also involves discussions with your coach to help change some of your behavior – how you interact with others – by practicing with your coach. Cognitive-Behavioral methods are very well respected and researched types of approach. They are known to be effective, even when you do a lot of the work on your own.

WHY A WORKBOOK?

Cognitive-Behavioral methods often use writing exercises to help us remember and strengthen our use of knowledge and new skills, as well as helping us practice them in person. It appears to help us build stronger pathways in our brains for solving problems more automatically in the future, just like practicing a sport or a musical instrument. This workbook belongs to you and is intended to be confidential, so you can refer back to it in the future to reinforce the skills you will learn.

The workbook also helps focus the coaching sessions, while leaving time for you to raise other issues during part of each session.

You may find it is easier to communicate and solve problems with others who have learned the same skills contained in this workbook, such as using the same methods for email responses and proposing solutions to problems.

Some of the writing exercises can be done before a coaching session, while most of them will be done during or after a coaching session. It helps to read ahead about the topic for the next session. Consult with your coach about any homework between sessions. The workbook is designed to help focus and remember your coaching discussions. It's up to you!

NOW, LET'S GET STARTED!

SESSION 1: PROBLEMS OR ISSUES TO DISCUSS

COACHING TIPS

As explained in the Introduction for the client, the *New Ways for Work™* method can be used with clients who were referred by management because of behavior problems or self-referred by a client who wants to solve a workplace problem or advance in his or her career. Clarifying which type of problem or issues you are dealing with will help you orient yourself in working with the client to be most effective. It may take the entire first session to clarify whether the client was referred by management or is self-referred. In either case, learning the skills contained in the Workbook will always be the client's responsibility.

GETTING ACQUAINTED

Since this is your first session, hold off on introducing the Workbook until you have gotten acquainted and performed any necessary assessment. The writing for the first session is not too long, as it is understood that you will need time to build rapport.

GETTING A HISTORY

This method assumes that you will use your existing skills and professional standards in obtaining a sufficient history or assessment of the client to appropriately address his or her Identified Problem or Issue. Don't let the Workbook interfere with this initial responsibility. The Workbook does not help you structure this preliminary aspect of your initial session.

INTRODUCING THE WORKBOOK

Depending on the nature of the referral, the client may be expected to use the Workbook or you may recommend the use of the Workbook. Our experience is that clients enjoy learning the skills in the Workbook and that they have positive success in using them after the sessions are over. You can explain that this is a "cognitive-behavioral" method and that such methods have had a lot of success in helping people help themselves.

WRITING IN THE WORKBOOK

Since most people think of coaching or counseling as an opportunity to sit and talk about problems, it may come as a surprise that this method focuses so much on writing exercises. It may be tempting to just verbally discuss the exercises, but it will be much better in the long run to encourage the client to "write that down in your Workbook," especially after a good thought or phrase has come to mind. Our experience is that clients get used to writing in the Workbook if you encourage them from the start and make it an easy exercise.

Some clients may ask you "What should I write?" Ask them to tell you out loud. Then encourage them to write what they said in the Workbook, or an abbreviated version of it. If they ask you for help, you might ask them to say it, then help them reframe it for the Workbook.

CONFIDENTIALITY OF THE WORKBOOK

Mention that the client owns the Workbook and should keep it confidential in a safe place. Go over the confidentiality standards of your profession which may apply. Make it clear to any "powers that be" that this is confidential and of no use to them. Any employer can purchase a copy of the blank Workbook, if they want to know what topics are discussed and how. Discuss any issues regarding possible access to the Workbook by subpoena in the event of a workplace legal issue.

For example, therapist's notes are confidential, but in some states they can be brought into a legal case if the client makes his or her own "mental state" an issue in a legal matter, such as a divorce or employment lawsuit. This is extremely rare, and the fact that the Workbook is the client's property kept in the client's own safe place should make it even more confidential than any therapist's notes. However, legal concerns or questions should be referred to a lawyer in your state.

DETERMINING THE NUMBER OF SESSIONS

Since this method is short-term and structured, it will help to clarify the intended number of sessions from the start, so you will both know how much of the Workbook you are covering. If you are an EAP or workplace coach, you may already know the number of sessions before you meet the client. If you are a therapist used to working with clients on an open-ended basis, you should determine the number of sessions you will use with this method – then you can discuss what to do later after these sessions are over. If you have less than 12 sessions, you can give the client tips for working through the Workbook on his or her own after you are done meeting.

IDENTIFIED PROBLEM OR ISSUE

Depending on why the client has come to you, the Identified Problem or Issue may be changing past behavior or wanting to learn new skills to advance in one's career. In either case, the client needs to "own" the problem and define it in a way that is comfortable and makes sense to him or her.

During this session, the client may discuss a general goal related to the Identified Problem or Issue, and that is fine. But don't have a focused, in-depth discussion of goals at this point. During Session 3, there will be a more focused discussion of specific "personal goals" under each of the four new ways skills, which will be introduced and explained in Session 2.

HOMEWORK AND PRACTICE CONVERSATIONS

If appropriate, you might suggest some homework for the client before the second session. You might even consider a practice conversation you could role-play, to help him or her prepare for an upcoming difficult situation in the coming week, related to the Identified Problem or Issue.

TRACKING THE WORKBOOK PAGES

The next few pages are exactly what the client sees in his or her Workbook. For your convenience, the Workbook page numbers are at the top of each of these pages. This way you can tell the client where to look and the client can tell you where he or she is when discussing a page. The Coaching Manual page numbers are at the bottom of each page of this manual.

New Ways for Work
Individual Coaching

SESSION 1: PROBLEMS OR ISSUES TO DISCUSS

During this session, you and your Employee Assistance Professional (EAP), counselor, or coach will get acquainted. He or she will ask you questions about the problems or issues you want to address in the coaching and also discuss your general goals for the coaching. You will also discuss how many sessions of *New Ways for Work* coaching you would like, up to 12 sessions.

Your coach will also ask some questions about your background, in order to more fully understand the problem or issue you want help with and where it fits into your life – including some of the challenges you have faced in the past that may help in coaching for the future. If you wish, you can prepare a written page or two about your background, or just wait to meet with your coach and talk about it.

PROBLEMS OR ISSUES TO DISCUSS

Write one to two problems or issues here that you would like to discuss with your Coach:

DEBBIE: *The Office Manager at my job treats me disrespectfully and makes it very difficult to work together.*

JOHN: *I made a comment to my co-worker and I was told to take this coaching.*

MARIA: *I want to move up in my company and it will help me to learn how to manage negative employee feedback and difficult employees.*

Pick one problem or issue and explain it in more detail. Let's call this your "Identified Problem" or "Issue":

DEBBIE: *I recently got a job as a medical receptionist. But the Office Manager, Jill, has problems. One minute she's friendly enough. The next minute she doesn't respond or cuts off the conversation. The other women in the office told me that two previous receptionists quite because of her. Jill's behavior continues to be provocative and demeaning, so I'm seeking outside counseling to decide what to do.*

JOHN: *This guy where I work, Zachary, made a nasty comment about my wife and I told him "I will deal with you after work." I never did anything, but he complained to our supervisor, who said I needed to get some coaching about not making threats at work.*

MARIA: *I want to become a department head at my tech company, which has mostly male employees. I've been a supervisor and I have been told that I could communicate better. Occasionally, an employee has complained that I'm too abrasive in how I talk to them. It was suggested that I work on communication skills that will work with these types of employees.*

Describe or discuss in general terms your initial thoughts about what your goal(s) are for the coaching in relation to the Identified Problem or Issue you have selected:

DEBBIE: *I want to know if there's a way I can get along with Jill, or if I should change jobs.*

JOHN: *I want to get along with Zach and my supervisor so there are no problems.*

MARIA: *I need to learn some less threatening ways of talking to men who are smart but not good at working together. I want them to respect me in the process.*

Describe or discuss what it would look like in your daily life, if you accomplished the goal(s) described above in relation to your Identified Problem or Issue:

DEBBIE: *I would be able to look forward to going to work and wouldn't have to worry about my supervisor's mood.*

JOHN: *I could be relaxed at work and joke around with Zach without worrying about getting into trouble.*

MARIA: *The men at work would treat me with respect and listen to my suggestions without getting defensive. The women at work would feel stronger because I am their supervisor.*

Think of anything else you would like to remember to tell your Coach in regard to your Identified Problem or Issue:

DEBBIE: *I really have empathy for Jill, as I understand she is raising her grandchildren because her daughter is a drug addict. But I don't want her to take it out on me.*

JOHN: *I think that Zachary should be required to have coaching too, since he made such a nasty remark about my wife. I don't think it's fair that he gets away with that, but that I get in trouble because I made a remark my supervisor thought was threatening. I didn't do anything.*

MARIA: *I have gotten good reviews from my boss, who has encouraged me to apply for higher positions in our company, because they want more women to work there and think that more women supervisors will help women feel comfortable about staying.*

SESSION SUMMARY

Write a key thought(s) that came out of this session that you would like to remember:

DEBBIE: *I have some hope that my counselor will help me figure out whether I can cope with Jill or need to get out of there. I'm interested in learning the skills my counselor has mentioned.*

JOHN: *I think this is stupid. But I guess since I'm here I'll try to get something out of it.*

MARIA: *I am encouraged to learn from my coach that I already have good skills I can strengthen with the techniques we will discuss. Also, that the communication skills I learn can also be taught to my employees to help them be more effective communicators.*

SESSION 2: THE 4 NEW WAYS SKILLS

COACHING TIPS

In this session, there is a lot of content information provided for your client regarding the four New Ways skills (*flexible thinking, managed emotions, moderate behavior,* and *checking yourself*). While the Workbook asks the client to discuss "why you think that flexible thinking is helpful or unhelpful, or in what types of situations it could be helpful or unhelpful," we are clearly saying it is better to use *flexible thinking.* The reason we want the client to think about this in terms of pros and cons is to get the client *reflecting* on these concepts rather than just being told which is better. This will assist in better understanding and better recall.

Part of why we present these four skills in such simple terms is that it is hard to remember what to do when emotions are running high and we are defensive in a given situation. This is often what clients are facing in the workplace, which drives them to seek assistance.

As most people know, when we are highly upset the more logical parts of our brains shut down and we switch into fight, flight or freeze mode. However, even in this self-protective mode of behavior, we can remember some simple phrases that have been repeated a lot. This is why we repeatedly talk about *flexible thinking, managed emotions, moderate behavior,* and *checking ourselves.* You can share this explanation with your client.

In terms of when *all-or-nothing thinking* or *extreme behavior* might be helpful, there are some times for clear and extreme action. An example would be if another worker didn't realize something was about to fall on him or her that could cause serious injury. Quick, aggressive action to push the worker out of the way could be very helpful, instead of taking the time to use flexible thinking to consider several options. However, this is a very rare circumstance in modern offices and workplaces, so flexible thinking and moderate behaviors are the more successful skills to use.

OTHER PEOPLE'S EXAMPLES

Throughout this Workbook, we start by asking the client to think of someone else in terms of how they think, manage emotions, and behave. This makes it slightly removed and easier for clients to learn the skills. Then, we progress to asking them to apply the concept to their own lives, when they have already started to apply the skill to another person's situation. So we often start with: "Someone You Know" or "Someone You Have Observed." Try to help the client take this approach, rather than pulling the conversation back to himself or herself prematurely.

COGNITIVE PRINCIPLES

A key concept throughout this Workbook is that how we think influences how we feel and behave. Therefore, the following diagram in the Workbook is an important one that you can refer to often:

ALL-OR-NOTHING THINKING:

"It's hopeless" → "Now I'm really angry" → Shoving papers off the desk
Compared to:

FLEXIBLE THINKING:

"There's more than one solution to this problem"
↓

"I don't feel as stressed"

↓

"I'm going to talk to someone about this deadline"

Once they get this concept - that you can change how you feel and behave, by changing how you think – you will have helped them tremendously, without having to go deep into the principles of cognitive therapy. This entire Workbook reinforces this simple concept over and over again.

DISCUSSING CONCEPTS

It's more important that the client understands the concepts surrounding one of these four skills than to rush through all of them. On the other hand, however, don't get stuck in a deep philosophical discussion of "why" they make sense. Keep the focus on "doing" the skills and writing about them.

HOMEWORK

This session had a lot of information. Having the client do the homework will help him or her absorb the lessons and practice the skills. This information is often very encouraging to clients, so that you can suggest that they consider trying it out in the coming week – at least in terms of observing others and themselves. If appropriate, you can even role-play a situation the client expects to face in the coming week.

Also, let the client know that others may or may not be excited to hear about these skills, so he or she should be cautious about trying to point out the insights they have about other people's behavior to them.

REALISTIC EXPECTATIONS FOR PROBLEM RESOLUTION

This question at the end of the session is designed to help the client think realistically about solving problems, rather than having "all-or-nothing" expectations. A lot of this method is to teach the client to self-reflect or at least shift the focus from others to him or herself.

SESSION 2: THE 4 NEW WAYS SKILLS

THE NEW WAYS SKILLS ARE:

Flexible Thinking

Managed Emotions

Moderate Behaviors

Checking Yourself

FLEXIBLE THINKING

We are constantly facing new situations that may never have occurred in our lives before, or even in the world before. One of the biggest barriers to success in a changing world is all-or-nothing thinking. What we need is flexible thinking for new ways of solving problems in new situations. All-or-nothing thinking keeps us stuck in old ways and over-reacting to change, while flexible thinking helps us keep thinking of new ideas and trying them out until something works.

HERE ARE SOME COMMON EXAMPLES OF ALL-OR-NOTHING THINKING:

"My life isn't working. I have to change everything that I do."

"I'm doing an excellent job. There's nothing I could improve."

"Everyone is against me. There's nothing I can do."

"Everyone should see things my way."

"I'm perfect as I am. There is nothing I can learn from this coach."

"Everything I do is wrong. This coach will save me."

"Things were wonderful. Now they're horrible!"

Write a *realistic* statement that is not "all-or-nothing thinking" that relates to your life:
For example: "I can learn new ways of doing things, regardless of how I did things in the past."
Or: "A co-worker may be able to change some of their workplace behavior, if I change mine. Let's see."

DEBBIE: I'm actually pretty happy in my life. This problem isn't the end of the world.

JOHN: I don't have to let things bother me so much. I can ignore a lot of what others do.

MARIA: I can move up in my career without having to be perfect.

Write a *realistic* statement that is not "all-or-nothing thinking" that relates to your Identified Problem or Issue:

DEBBIE: I don't have to let my supervisor problem ruin my life. It's just a problem to solve.

JOHN: I can ignore what Zach says without feeling that I have to prove anything to him.

MARIA: I'm actually doing quite well in my career so far. I'm in a great company.

Discuss with your coach why you think that flexible thinking is helpful or unhelpful, or in what types of situations it could be helpful or unhelpful. Write an example of when flexible thinking could be helpful in addressing your Identified Problem or Issue:

DEBBIE: I can be flexible in my thinking about my supervisor. Even though I have empathy for her problems at home, doesn't mean I can't speak up and try to improve my own situation.

JOHN: I know it's good to be flexible, but I can only stand so much when other people make comments. It would be helpful to tell myself I don't have to react to everything.

MARIA: I can enjoy my job and think about how to help my employees communicate better, rather than fearing their criticism.

Discuss with your coach a statement you can practice to remind yourself to use flexible thinking in the future, and a situation where you can practice flexible thinking this week. Write the statement here. Keep it short and easy to remember.

DEBBIE: I'm okay. Her problems are not about me.

JOHN: I will try to think of something else when Zach bothers me.

MARIA: I'm excited about learning new skills – I'm open-minded.

THINK, FEEL, ACT

Flexible thinking is at the center of managing emotions and keeping our behavior moderate. Many cognitive scientists believe that our thoughts lead to our emotions, which then leads to our behavior. With this in mind, you may be able to change how you feel and how you act, by simply changing how you *think* about something.

For example, Paul is facing a tight deadline on a project this week. He feels stressed and starts thinking it's hopeless to meet this deadline, then he starts feeling angry about his workload in general and he shoves the papers on his desk onto the floor. Paul's *all-or-nothing* thinking led him to feel angry, which led him to feel so frustrated that he shoved his papers – which will take a while to re-organize and make it harder to get done on time.

Instead, suppose that Paul had responded to his thinking that "it's hopeless," by telling himself to use his *flexible thinking* – that there's more than one solution to most problems and thinking about what alternatives he might have. He could say one or more of the following to himself:

Who can I talk to about changing the deadline?

Is there someone who could help me finish the project on time?

Can I change my priorities to make more room for this project this week?

I want to meet this deadline, but it's not the end of the world and it's not worth throwing things around and stressing myself out.

Just thinking about these alternatives will usually calm him down. He *feels* better because of these thoughts, which help him feel less hopeless. Not perfect, of course, but less hopeless. Now, he can look at how to solve his problem rather than just over-reacting and feeling worse and behaving badly. Here's how this looks in terms of influencing his own feelings and behavior by how he tells himself to think:

ALL-OR-NOTHING THINKING:

"It's hopeless" → "Now I'm really angry" → Shoving papers off the desk
Compared to:

FLEXIBLE THINKING:

"There's more than one solution to this problem"

"I don't feel as stressed"

"I'm going to talk to someone about this deadline"

As you can see, simply changing what you think (what you tell yourself – often known as your "self-talk") can make a huge difference in how you feel and how you behave.

SOMEONE YOU KNOW

Think of someone in your life who often uses all-or-nothing thinking. Write an example of what he/she would say or think.

DEBBIE: My supervisor is easily distracted and irritable. She thinks everything is overwhelming.

JOHN: I have a friend who always says "That person deserves to die" when he's watching a show or watching the news. I think that's pretty extreme.

MARIA: One of my employees speaks in extremely disrespectful terms: "That's the stupidest idea I've ever heard" he says frequently.

Write a new flexible thinking way that he/she could speak or think in the future on this subject:

DEBBIE: She could say "I'm doing a lot for my granddaughters and don't have to walk around feeling stressed all the time."

JOHN: He could just say "That person's a jerk" and then talk about something else.

MARIA: Instead, he could say: "I don't think that idea will work. Here's why."

Remember, this is just a practice exercise to help you learn new ways of flexible thinking. So don't really tell the other person to think differently. That's their job. Focus on yourself now.

YOURSELF

Think of an example of all-or-nothing thinking you have sometimes. Write them here:

DEBBIE: My job is hopeless. My supervisor is a total jerk.

JOHN: I can't let anybody say anything bad about my family - I have to prove they're wrong.

MARIA: I'll never make progress in a tech company – I should just switch to another field.

Write a flexible way that you could speak or think differently from what you wrote above:

DEBBIE: My job is not hopeless. There's a lot I like about it. My supervisor is one part of it.

JOHN: I don't have to care about what other people say – I can choose to ignore them.

MARIA: I've made a lot of progress in this tech company – I've gotten this far.

MANAGED EMOTIONS

Upset emotions are normal in threatening situations no matter where you are, who you are, or who you are with. Yet being unable to manage our upset emotions can distract us from achieving our goals and create new problems for us, such as with those around us. Unmanaged emotions can make our lives a lot worse – even in just a split second. So learning to manage our emotions – even when times are tense – can make a big difference in our success at work. Learning how to stay calm in a crisis or how to calm yourself down after a stressful moment can make a huge difference in today's work world.

Here are some examples of unmanaged emotions that get people into trouble:

Yelling at co-workers.

Making threats to hurt someone on the job.

Bursting into tears around co-workers.

Refusing to cooperate with a manager out of anger.

Yelling at a difficult customer out of frustration.

Giving the silent treatment to a supervisor or co-worker.

Think of an example when you managed your emotions in a stressful situation. Write them down here:

DEBBIE: I wanted to yell at my supervisor "Don't just walk away while we're talking," but I held my tongue. I'm not ready to get fired.

JOHN: I wanted to punch Zach after what he said, but I didn't.

MARIA: I felt very defensive after one of my employees said I didn't understand technology. But I just waited to speak to my supervisor who said I actually know a lot and to ignore his comment.

Now, think of a situation in regard to your Identified Problem or Issue when you were under stress and you didn't manage your emotions very well. Write it here:

DEBBIE: I once mumbled under my breath that Jill was an a—hole, and she asked what I said. I said it was nothing, but it was a very awkward moment.

JOHN: I sometimes tell people "I'll deal with you after work" if they say something I don't like. This is the first time I've gotten into trouble because of it. I guess I should say nothing when I'm upset.

MARIA: I burst into tears once after one of my software engineers told me I didn't belong there. He could see me when he left my office.

ONE WAY TO MANAGE OUR EMOTIONS

Tell yourself an encouraging statement

In the Olympics, most of the athletes learn to tell themselves encouraging statements while they are in the middle of extremely difficult challenges and millions of people are watching, especially when things are going badly and they are feeling very stressed or upset. These statements help them keep their cool.

Think of an encouraging statement you can tell yourself to get through an upsetting time related to your Identified Problem or Issues:

For example: "You can do it!"

Or: "I got through a worse situation last year! I'll get through this too!"

Write down one or more that you like:

DEBBIE: I've never had a supervisor like this before. It's not about me – it's about her.

JOHN: It doesn't matter what other people think or say. I'm cool with how I am already.

MARIA: The tech field has some gender problems. I'm going to make a difference.

Think of a stressful situation in the coming week in regard to your Identified Problem or Issue when telling yourself this encouraging statement might help you stay calm. **Discuss it with your coach.**

MODERATE BEHAVIORS

In the modern work world, moderate behaviors help us the most. Extreme behaviors can make things worse. You could have to spend a lot of time trying to fix the damage of extreme behaviors. Even extreme behavior in response to someone else's extreme behavior can make things worse. Here are some examples of extreme behaviors:

Insulting a customer

Insulting a manager

Insulting a co-worker

Storming out of a room in anger

Pushing a co-worker

Throwing something at a co-worker

Threatening to hit a co-worker

Destroying company property

Stealing from the company

Writing a nasty email to anyone at work

Give an example of how an extreme behavior got someone into trouble:

DEBBIE: I have a friend who walked off a job once and regretted it afterwards.

JOHN: I know a guy who made a joke about bombs at an airport and got pulled aside and searched and questioned, and missed his plane because of it.

MARIA: One of our employees took a laptop home with top secret design information and was fired because of it.

Think of an example of how you used a moderate behavior when you *felt* like using an extreme behavior. Write it here:

DEBBIE: I once felt like quitting my job, but instead I took a walk around the building and calmed down.

JOHN: My neighbor and I almost got into a fight once, but my wife said to come inside so I did.

MARIA: At a meeting once I felt like interrupting the presenter because he made a remark, but I decided it would be better to talk to him about it privately afterward. So that's what I did.

Think of a situation related to your Identified Problem or Issue that's coming up soon in which you may be tempted to use an extreme behavior. Think of a moderate behavior you could use instead and write it here:

DEBBIE: I'm having a meeting with Jill this week and I'm feeling tempted to tell her she's a hostile b----. Instead, I will focus on listening to what she has to say and responding respectfully.

JOHN: My manager wants to talk to me about my future in our team and I want to tell him he has no business talking to me about this – I've worked there longer than he has. But I think I will just practice saying "I like this team and I'd like to continue working with everyone here – even Zachary. I've already apologized and it won't happen again."

MARIA: I have a project meeting this week about deadlines and I feel like just telling everyone they're doing a lousy job – since we're behind. Instead, I'll tell them about our new deadline and ask for their analysis of our delays and how to speed things up.

CHECKING YOURSELF

From time to time, ask yourself if you are using these skills:

Flexible Thinking

Managed Emotions

Moderate Behavior

It's easy to forget to use these skills in the middle of discussing problems or difficult situations. If you are facing a change, it can help to remind yourself to use these skills going into a situation – to "Check Yourself."

HOMEWORK

Select another problem from your Identified Problem or Issue list, or come up with a new one. We will use this problem to help you practice the skills we have been discussing.

DEBBIE: One of my co-workers wants to get together for dinner and a movie and I'm feeling uncomfortable and don't know how to say "No" to her without creating a problem at work.

John: My supervisor is a jerk about when we take vacations. I have a particular week I want to go to a family reunion and I think he'll say it's too early for him to make a commitment – then if I wait, he'll say it's too late and someone else gets that week.

MARIA: There's a young woman on our team who's been coming to work late. She has great skills and ideas, so she feels entitled. I want to prepare myself to confront her behavior without upsetting her.

All-or-nothing thoughts concerning this problem would be:

DEBBIE: This co-worker will bad-mouth me to everyone else on our team.

JOHN: I know my supervisor will say "No."

MARIA: She'll quit and blame it on me.

Flexible thoughts concerning this problem are:

DEBBIE: I'm already ambivalent about this job, so if she's really inappropriate it may help me decide to leave.

JOHN: I won't know until I ask for the vacation week.

MARIA: She has worked there for several years and is unlikely to quit.

In relation to this problem, an example of unmanaged emotions would be:

DEBBIE: If I yelled at her.

JOHN: If I yelled at him.

MARIA: If I avoided talking to her out of fear.

In relation to this problem, examples of managed emotions would be:

DEBBIE: If I calmly spoke to her and let her know it's a busy time for me so I'm not available.

JOHN: If I just asked for the vacation week and don't get angry if he says to wait. I'll just ask again a couple days later – and then a couple days later after that.

MARIA: If I stayed friendly and asked her to talk about the lateness problem first.

An example of extreme behavior in relation to this problem could be:

DEBBIE: If I told her she is over-stepping our work boundaries and to leave me alone.

JOHN: If I told everyone at work what a jerk our supervisor is.

MARIA: If I just started out intensely criticizing her.

An example of moderate behavior in relation to this problem on my part would be:

DEBBIE: If I just kept the conversation very brief and just said I'm busy for a while.

JOHN: If I looked into the personnel policy about vacations before I spoke with my supervisor.

MARIA: If I explained there was a problem we needed to talk about and I was interested in helping her solve it.

An encouraging statement that would help me in handling this problem successfully is:

DEBBIE: I can get through this. If she has a negative reaction, it's not about me.

JOHN: There's a policy about this and I'll just calmly follow the policy.

MARIA: I want to help her succeed, so I can be patient with her.

A realistic expectation for problem resolution in regard to this issue is:

1. 50% IMPROVEMENT

2. 20% IMPROVEMENT

3. 10% IMPROVEMENT

Explain why you selected the percentage you did.

DEBBIE: 10%. I don't know this co-worker very well, so I am slightly more hopeful but not certain if my approach will be well-received by her.

JOHN: 50%. I can convince him to follow the policy and give me my vacation.

MARIA: 20%. This employee does have a lateness problem, so I'm not expecting a lot, but I think my approach of having her talk first should help her stay less defensive.

REMEMBER TO BRING THIS HOMEWORK TO YOUR NEXT SESSION!

SESSION 3: REVIEW AND PERSONAL GOALS

COACHING TIPS

If you are only meeting for three sessions, this is the last session. However, you can still teach the client a lot of self-resilience and self-awareness in just these three sessions. If you have more sessions, you will have laid a good groundwork for future skills learning.

HOMEWORK

The discussion of the Homework from Session 2 will be very helpful because it is training for the coming weeks ahead for the client – either on his or her own, or for the future sessions with you as the coach.

Remember, the client might not have done the Homework, as predicted for some in the Introduction to this Coaching Manual. Don't let that become a power struggle or show frustration. Instead, do it briefly with the client in the beginning of this session, so that the concepts can be absorbed to some extent. This will be the basis of the client setting his or her own personal goals for the future in each of these four areas.

REVIEWING AND SETTING SOME PERSONAL GOALS

In this section we list four goals, which may seem familiar. However, the fourth goal is not "checking yourself," but rather:

"4. To validate my own strengths and personal qualities."

The reason for this is to help give the client encouragement to learn these skills and make one of these personal goals very easy and self-affirming. We have seen the need for a balance in setting goals, so that they don't become overwhelming or too far of a stretch for the client. By having the client set the personal goal of giving himself or herself validation, it will help them accomplish the other goals.

THINK OF PERSONAL GOALS FOR YOURSELF

These are meant to be easy goals to define, so there is no standard such as professionals have for setting organizational goals or educational "learning objectives." Instead, the only requirement is that it is something that the person could conceivably accomplish and not something for someone else to accomplish.

For example, some clients say:

"I want to use flexible thinking to convince my manager to treat me with respect."

This is not a goal over which the client could potentially have control. Instead, the client might write:

"I want to use flexible thinking to consider more options when my manager treats me disrespectfully."

This is a goal which the client could accomplish. The client could consider the option of practicing responses which might *influence* the manager to behave differently. But if that didn't work, the client might consider transferring to a different department or changing jobs. All of these are within the client's potential control. That's all that is needed in defining these personal goals.

THE FUTURE

If this is your client's last session, you can discuss how he or she might practice the four skills you have discussed in order to reach these goals. Since "Checking Yourself" isn't listed as one of the goals, encourage them to plan when and how they will reflect on whether or not they are using these skills.

You can also direct the client's attention to read the information and do the exercises in the next several sessions. There are a lot of good, simple skills that can be learned – even on one's own.

You can further show your client the worksheets in the back of the Workbook. While the first one ("Full Method Worksheet") may seem overwhelming or confusing, the second one ("Check Yourself – Checklist") is certainly easy to use right away. The first worksheet will make more sense after the client has read through the material in the other sessions.

If you are continuing on with your client, then these Personal Goals can be used as a reference point as you go through the next sessions, which emphasize specific smaller skills which help implement the four new ways skills.

SESSION 3: REVIEW AND PERSONAL GOALS

HOMEWORK

Discuss with your coach the homework from the previous session. Write down three key things you learned from your discussion:

_____

_____

_____

_____

_____

_____

_____

_____

_____

_____

REVIEWING AND SETTING SOME PERSONAL GOALS

Whether this is your last session or you are continuing with more sessions, this will be a review of what you have learned so far and an opportunity to plan for the future. This session ends with setting personal goals to help you apply these skills to your own situation in the future.

The following are four General Goals for you to think about, so that you can write down some Personal Goals for yourself to go under each one:

To use flexible thinking in dealing with difficult situations.

To manage my upset emotions during difficult situations.

To use moderate behaviors with other employees and managers.

To validate my own strengths and personal qualities.

HERE'S A LIST OF SOME IDEAS FOR PERSONAL GOALS:

"To practice flexible thinking when a co-worker is blaming me."

"To manage my emotions when a manager is publically criticizing my actions."

"To respond with moderate behaviors when my customers send angry emails."

"To get my team to listen to me when I make workplace suggestions."

"To protect my team from other people's comments and behavior."

Think of Personal Goals for Yourself, under each of the General Goals below. Discuss your ideas with your coach, then write a Personal Goal under each General Goal.

Then, write something you have already learned under each goal.

To use flexible thinking in dealing with difficult situations.

My personal goal:

DEBBIE: To use flexible thinking to come up with good choices about my job future.

JOHN: To use flexible thinking in deciding whether to respond to others' comments.

MARIA: To use flexible thinking in learning new ways of managing difficult employees.

What I have learned so far:

DEBBIE: That I already have several options for my job: ways to stay or leave.

JOHN: To say something else other than "I'll deal with you after work".

MARIA: To use flexible thinking in listening to employees views first when I have to address a performance problem with them and to stay open-minded.

To manage my upset emotions during difficult situations.

My personal goal:

DEBBIE: To give myself encouraging statements before difficult conversations.

JOHN: To take a break if someone says a nasty comment – or to just say nothing.

MARIA: To remind myself that I'm in this for the long-term, so I don't need to get upset with each little confrontation. I can meet the challenges of today's tech workforce.

What I have learned so far:

DEBBIE: That I'm not really emotionally upset knowing I have choices.

JOHN: That I can avoid getting upset when other people say stupid things.

MARIA: I'm already doing very well!

To use moderate behaviors with other employees, managers and clients/customers.

My personal goal:

DEBBIE: To avoid getting into direct confrontations with my Office Manager.

JOHN: To avoid saying threatening things, even if I don't mean them.

MARIA: To stay calm and not burst into tears when I'm criticized.

What I have learned so far:

DEBBIE: That I can remind myself that she has problems so it's not about me.

JOHN: That I can keep my mouth shut when I should, most of the time now.

MARIA: That I'm already doing very well! Criticism is just part of the job.

To validate my own strengths and personal qualities.

My personal goal:

DEBBIE: To remind myself that I'm good at learning and I'm a hard worker.

JOHN: To remember that I'm good at my job and they don't want to fire me.

MARIA: To believe that I'm a good supervisor, that I know the tech side of our business, that they need me and that I can make a difference in this company.

What I have learned so far:

DEBBIE: That I can solve this problem and I'm halfway there just realizing this.

JOHN: That I've stayed out of trouble since my stupid comment to Zachary.

MARIA: I'm already starting to believe these things.

REALISTIC EXPECTATIONS

Discuss with your coach a reasonable expectation for utilizing these four skills with your Identified Problem or Issue in the future.

How much do you think your situation will improve? _____ 50% _____ 20% _____ 10%

Discuss with your coach why 100% improvement is not realistic.

If you are finishing your coaching sessions with this third session, discuss how you can remember your goals for the future – especially in terms of your Identified Problem or Issue.

THE FUTURE

Discuss with your coach how you picture yourself using these skills in the future. Discuss how you will "Check Yourself" from time to time to remember to use these skills when you are under stress.

Write something you learned from this discussion:

DEBBIE: I can remind myself to be flexible, managed and moderate before I go to work each day, to avoid getting too stressed in the first place.

JOHN: I don't think I'll need to use these skills in the future. I'm just going to avoid responding when someone else says something stupid at work. I'll manage my emotions and behavior that way.[John's coaching ends after 3 sessions, so no more sample answers for him.]

MARIA: I'm going to remember to use flexible thinking in deciding how to respond to negative feedback. I'm going to manage my emotions by reminding myself "I already am doing a good job under the circumstances." I'm going to remind myself each day to keep my behavior moderate because I am in this for the long run, so that I can make a difference!

If you are going to have more sessions, throughout *New Ways for Work* you and your coach can look back on these personal goals to see if you are learning what you want to learn. You can change or add to these goals if something more meaningful comes up in the coaching. The goals are meant to guide you, not rule your life. But remember, these are your goals, so make sure to bring them up in your discussions of the skills described in this manual in each session.

Congratulations! You have finished three sessions of *New Ways for Work* coaching!

SESSION 4: FLEXIBLE THINKING: MAKING PROPOSALS

COACHING TIPS

The scenarios at the beginning of the session help reinforce the differences between *all-or-nothing thinking* and *flexible thinking*. This will help you know how much the client has absorbed this concept. You may need to reinforce the benefits of *flexible thinking,* or this may be a very simple concept for the client and you can move on quickly to Making Proposals. We don't provide sample answers for these scenarios as the focus is the most basic concept of identifying the differences between *all-or-nothing thinking* and *flexible thinking,* which we hope the client understands by now.

MAKING PROPOSALS

One of the key concepts of flexible thinking is that there is more than one solution to almost every problem. Therefore, offering and considering different proposals is one of the most important skills to learn for today's workplace. Employees and managers who value other's proposals will be more effective and have happier people around them. When there are lots of conflicts in a work group, it is usually because one or more people have a hard time tolerating different points of view.

It's really simple: In conflicts between two or more people, it usually helps to offer a proposal or ask for a proposal. Not only does it help solve problems by involving those who are closest to the problem, but it's also a good way to manage high-conflict situations. Having one or more employees *thinking* about proposals is much better than having them reacting and over-reacting to each other's behavior. It's hard to be angry when you're thinking about making proposals. If your client is a manager or someone who wants to become a manager, teaching them to stay calm and ask for proposals will help in many difficult situations.

Here are some additional tips to help your client with each of the steps of making proposals:

STEP 1: MAKING A PROPOSAL

This takes some thought but can be learned quickly with practice. One way to practice is to ask your client what proposals might have helped in each of the scenarios at the beginning of this Session 4.

STEP 2: ASKING AND ANSWERING QUESTIONS

If your client is dealing with a conflict with another employee, the other employee may quickly say "No" to a proposal. Encourage your client not to be rattled by that response, but instead to ask the other person for a proposal: "So, what's your proposal?" It's recommended to do this with a calm tone of voice, which may calm the other person too. Then asking questions about the other person's proposal can help keep the focus on discussing details and ideas, rather than on emotional reactions.

One of the big tips here is to discourage "Why" questions. But this doesn't have to be absolute. In a heated discussion, "why" questions are usually criticisms, but in calm conversations "why" questions can really be innocent questions and don't need to be prohibited.

If there are two employees in a conflict or there is a group meeting about a difficult subject, proposals and questions can lead quickly to a "No" response. In this case, a manager or outside consultant or mediator can slow the process down and say:

"Ask some questions about each other's proposals so that we can see what might lead to a mutually-agreeable decision. The more you understand each other's proposals, the more likely you are to come to an agreement. The more I understand each of your proposals, the more I will be able to help you make new proposals that can reach an agreement."

STEP 3

By keeping responses focused on "Yes," "No," or "I'll think about it," the tendency to get into criticisms can be managed. An employee who learns how to say one of these responses will keep it simple and avoid getting real upset. A manager who can encourage such responses will be seen as one who is skilled at managing conflicts.

It helps to know that "I'll think about it" is often an easy way to save face and that this option helps people agree later on, rather than looking like they were caving in on the spot to the other's proposal.

For more on teaching skills for making and responding to proposals in the workplace (or anywhere), see the book *So, What's Your Proposal?* by Bill Eddy (HighConflictInstitutePress.com). There is also a Webinar on the subject of teaching clients to make proposals at www.HighConflictInstitute.com.

EXAMPLE OF A PROPOSAL DISCUSSION (RAPHAEL'S PROPOSAL)

This example helps show the rhythm of the three steps above. You might even read the second example (the more positive one) out loud, with you playing the supervisor role, and ask your client how it felt to have a proposal seriously considered.

YOURSELF

After your client writes a couple proposals and offers questions that could be asked about them under "Yourself", see if your client wants to role-play that scenario or do another one for "Practice with your coach."

PRACTICE WITH YOUR COACH

Remember to follow the three steps of Proposal, Questions and Answers, then Response. Have your client play the difficult person in their example and you play the client. Then, switch roles. Depending on your client, you may want to help the client cope with hearing lots of questions and then a "No" for a while, but staying in the discussion. Then, after some more proposals and questions, try to end by saying "Yes." This can make it a satisfying and realistic process, which gives your client confidence as well as flexibility.

SESSION 4: FLEXIBLE THINKING: MAKING PROPOSALS
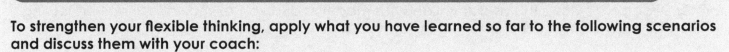

To strengthen your flexible thinking, apply what you have learned so far to the following scenarios and discuss them with your coach:

Joe (who has an excellent attendance record) was ten minutes late to work one morning when one of his most important customers called. Mary, the receptionist, took the call and told the customer she had no idea where Joe was and transferred the call to a rival sales associate. Was this all-or- nothing thinking? If so, what could Mary have done that would show flexible thinking?

Write your responses here:

_____

_____

_____

_____

Alice and Robert worked very hard together on developing an important PowerPoint presentation for their agency. Alice was not comfortable speaking before groups. Robert suggested that he do all the presentations, however he wanted only his name to appear on the PowerPoint title page. Does Robert's proposal show all-or-nothing thinking? If so, what could Robert have done that would show flexible thinking?

Write your responses here:

_____

_____

_____

_____

Margaret was trying to learn a new software program and was having trouble with the billing function. The office assistant had mastered the new program and offered to help to anyone who needed it. Margaret thought that if she asked for help she would be viewed as incompetent. Does Margaret show all-or-nothing thinking? If so, how could Margaret respond with flexible thinking?

Write your responses here:

_____

_____

_____

Jack, the new Agency Director, believes his management staff should have no contact with the former Director. His views this as disloyal and has made his displeasure known. Is this all-or-nothing thinking? If so, what would be flexible thinking for Jack?

Write your responses here:

_____

_____

_____

MAKING PROPOSALS

In Session 2 we talked about how flexible thinking can help you choose how you feel. You're not stuck with just one feeling about any situation – you can actually decide how you are going to feel to a great extent by what you tell yourself.

Another aspect of flexible thinking is deciding how to resolve a conflict with someone at work. As we said in Session 2, there is more than one solution to most problems. You can consider alternatives by making a list, making a proposal, or asking for a proposal from the other person in the conflict. Realizing and practicing this helps avoid just reacting to what someone else says or does.

3 STEPS OF MAKING PROPOSALS

One of the simplest ways to deal with another person in a conflict at work or making decisions is to respectfully ask him or her to make a proposal – or offering your own proposal. Here's a way to handle making proposals in three steps:

Step 1:   Make a proposal

Step 2:   Ask and answer questions about the proposal

Step 3:   Respond with: "Yes." "No." Or: "I'll think about it."

Here's how you can handle each step:

STEP 1:   MAKE A PROPOSAL

Ideally, proposals will include:

> Who does
>
> What,
>
> When and
>
> Where.

For example: "I propose that we each take a turn at cleaning up the snack area and the refrigerator – that we have a weekly schedule, with each of us taking a day."

This is much better than saying: "You never cleaned up the snack area! You don't even realize how much I clean up after you! I want some respect here for all that I've done!"

And then the other staff members get angry back: "You always want to be in charge of everything – even the snack area." And on and on.

Can you see how it would have been so much simpler for the person to just ask for what he or she wanted in the future by making a proposal? It saves all of the blame and defensiveness that people get stuck in, when talking about the past.

Proposals are always about the future. They are not about the past or about the other person's intentions or *Why* they made the proposal. *Why* questions easily turn into a criticism of the other person's proposal.

"*Why* did you say that?" really means "I think that's a stupid idea and I want to force you to admit it." Instead, if you think the other person's proposal is a bad idea, then the best thing to do is to just make another proposal – until you can both agree on something.

STEP 2: ASK AND ANSWER QUESTIONS ABOUT THE PROPOSAL

After one person has made a proposal, the other person may not be sure whether they can agree or not. Therefore, it often helps to ask questions. One of the best questions is to ask "What would your proposal look like in action?" This way you can get clearer on the Who, What, Where and When of the proposal. You might even ask: "What's your picture of how this would work? What would you do? What would I do, if you could picture your proposal actually happening?"

But of course, you don't want to ask "Why" questions, because that usually starts up the defensiveness. And if someone's defensiveness is triggered, then it makes it hard for them to think of solutions to problems. Watch out for challenging questions about a proposal, like "How do you expect me to do that?" "What were you thinking when you came up with that idea?" "You know you never did that before." "Don't you realize that our boss will never go along with that?" All of these create the same problems as "Why" questions, because they are about criticisms and defensiveness, not true questions about how to *implement* the proposal.

STEP 3: RESPOND WITH "YES." "NO." OR: "I'LL THINK ABOUT IT."

Once you've heard a proposal and asked any questions about it, all you have to do to respond is to say: "Yes." "No." Or: "I'll think about it." You always have the right to say any one of these. Of course, there are consequences to each choice, but you always have these three choices at least. Here's some examples of each:

YES: "Yes, I agree. Let's do that." And then stop! No need to save face, evaluate the other person's proposal, or give the other person some negative feedback. Just let it go. After all, if you have been personally criticized or attacked, it's not about you.

Personal attacks are not problem-solving. They are about the person making the hostile attack. You are better off to ignore everything else. Of course, if your agreement on this issue is being written up, there may be some more details to discuss – which may lead to more proposals about those details.

NO: "No, I don't want to change the current system. I'll try to make other arrangements to solve this problem. Let's keep the system as is." Just keep it simple. Avoid the urge to defend your decision or criticize the other person's idea. You said "No." You're done. Let it drop. Think about your next proposal.

I'LL THINK ABOUT IT: "I'm not sure about your proposal - I'll need to think about it. I'll get back to you tomorrow about your idea. Right now I have to get back to work. Thanks for making a proposal." Once again, just stop the discussion there. Avoid the temptation to discuss it at length, or question the validity of the other person's point of view. It is what it is.

When you say "I'll think about it," you are respecting the other person. It calms people to know you are taking them seriously enough to think about what they said. This doesn't mean you will agree. It just means you'll think about it. It helps to say a time when you will get back to the other person with your decision, such as: "I'll get back to you tomorrow – or Friday by 5pm."

Make a New Proposal: If there isn't an agreement after the 3 steps above, then the burden shifts to the respondent who said "No." Now that person needs to make a new proposal. Perhaps that person will think of a new approach that neither person thought of before. Encourage him or her to propose anything. (Remind them that there are consequences to each proposal.) And the other person can always respond: "Yes." "No." or "I'll think about it." (There are consequences to each of those responses, too.)

Discuss with your coach the benefits or problems you see in using this approach to making proposals.

Then, analyze the following situation:

EXAMPLE OF A PROPOSAL DISCUSSION

Raphael's Proposal: "I want to change my hours to a later shift. I'm having a hard time getting my daughter to school and getting to work on time."

Supervisor's Questions: "What hours are you proposing? And why do you think that's even an option?"

Raphael's Answer: "Look, you don't have to get snotty about it! I'm proposing I start an hour later and leave an hour later."

Supervisor's Response: "I was thinking about how I could persuade my boss to allow us to do your proposal, but if you talk to me that way, I'm not even going to try."

Are Raphael and his supervisor following the proposal method we just described? NO

Write down at least 2 things that are going wrong in this discussion and discuss them with your coach:

The Supervisor asked a "Why?" question, which was really an insulting remark.

Raphael is returning the insult by saying the Supervisor is "getting snotty about it." This isn't a straight question and a straight answer.

Would the following be a better discussion for Raphael and his supervisor?

Raphael's Proposal: "I want to change my hours to a later shift. I'm having a hard time getting my daughter to school and getting to work on time."

Supervisor's Questions: "What hours are you proposing?"

Raphael's Answer: "I'm proposing I start an hour later and leave an hour later."

Supervisor's Response: "I'll think about it. I have to see if my boss will allow us to make a change like this. I'll get back to you by Friday morning."

Discuss with your coach why this may be a better approach than the one above.

Write something you learned from this discussion.

It's tempting to give an insulting remark in response to a request or proposal, but it doesn't help anything.

YOURSELF

Think of a situation you are currently facing. Write two different proposals which might help in this situation:

DEBBIE:
I suggest that I reduce my hours by 4-8 hours per week, depending on how business is going.

Since we tend to be slow mid-week, I propose that I specifically take off Wednesdays all day or work a half-day.

MARIA:
I propose that our team have a training in communication techniques, such as making proposals, responding to hostile emails and managing our emotions with encouraging statements.

I propose that I meet with each individual on our team and teach them a few communication techniques that will help them be heard more effectively.

Now think of two questions that you might get asked about either proposal, and how you would answer them:

For DEBBIE (Regarding her Proposal #1):
When would you need to know which day would be a half day or a day off?
Would this be permanent or temporary?

For MARIA (Regarding her Proposal #2):
Would the individual meetings be at the time of annual reviews?
What specific types of communication problems will you be trying to address?

PRACTICE WITH YOUR COACH

Use your coach to practice a difficult conversation you might face in the coming week, in which a proposal might help you manage the situation. Practice having the conversation with your coach: First, with you playing the other person and your coach responding as you. Then, have your coach play the other person and you respond for yourself – calmly making a proposal to address the situation.

Write what you learned from practicing a proposal discussion with your coach:

DEBBIE: I learned that it is acceptable to make proposals to one's supervisor and that they can just be called suggestions or proposals.

MARIA: I learned that I can make a difference for our team by thinking and making proposals about what to do in the long run, rather than just reacting to problems and stress.

HOMEWORK

Think of another situation you are facing with a potentially difficult person. Think of a proposal you could make to handle that situation and write it here.

_____

_____

_____

Then, think of what the other person would say or ask in response to your proposal:

_____

_____

_____

_____

Then, write how you could respond to that with a revised proposal:

_____

_____

_____

_____

OUTCOME

If you actually made a proposal with a difficult person during the week, write down how it went. Then, discuss this the next time you meet with your coach.

_____

_____

_____

_____

Making proposals can take practice, but it's a good way to solve problems and also a good way to calm a conflict by focusing yourself and the other person on solutions rather than blame and frustration.

SESSION 5: MANAGED EMOTIONS: CALMING YOURSELF

COACHING TIPS

REVIEWING HOMEWORK

When reviewing homework with your client, let the client take the lead in analyzing what he or she has written. Avoid jumping in with advice. Ask questions about what they learned and/or what questions they have. Then, give your input.

MANAGED EMOTIONS

The need to manage one's emotions is a topic that will be obvious to many clients, but one of the hardest to deal with for others. There is a popular belief that upset emotions have to be vented one way or another. Some clients will claim that this means keeping feelings "bottled up inside" and that they can't tolerate how that feels. But keeping in mind the diagram in Session 2, how we think can significantly influence how we feel. Therefore, we can generally reduce how upset we feel inside more by changing our thinking than by venting our feelings. You may need to explain this a few times to some clients.

CALMING YOUR UPSET EMOTIONS

ENCOURAGING STATEMENTS

You may recognize the method in the Workbook instructions as giving yourself "affirmations." This is a simple but powerful approach using more familiar words for the client. Feel free to call these affirmations and suggest other resources which talk about affirmations, if you have a client who may be interested doing more with this concept.

YOUR "STAR"

This is another term we have developed to make it simple for remembering

Statements **T**hat **A**re **R**einforcing to the client. You can suggest that they think about using their STAR to give them guidance, like a sailor keeping an eye on the North STAR to get through a dark night.

TAKING A BREAK

When we have upset emotions we have stress hormones pumping through our bodies. It's common knowledge that it takes a few minutes to flush these hormones out of our system as we calm down – typically 20 to 30 minutes. Then we can think more clearly again.

Practice with your client having him or her say "I need a break for a few minutes." Often people realize that would help, but they are uncomfortable asking for a break. Role-playing their supervisor or a customer may help your client get more comfortable saying this is what they need. Generally, the more confident a person is when making a request, the more likely that person will get what they requested.

Talking to someone who is not involved.

When people are upset, it's a natural tendency to want to get support and agreement for their point of view. Unfortunately, this often just makes things worse. Instead, speaking with someone who is not involved will usually help someone calm down until they can think more clearly.

Your client may wonder why it's not okay to speak with someone who agrees with him or her. The problem with this is that it doesn't help give them perspective or calm emotions. It often results in increasing the conflict, if a person agrees and takes sides. They often want to participate in a demanding way that may involve confronting others who will actually think more negatively of the target. While it might seem in the moment like a wonderful idea, it often results in more controversy and negative opinions by others about the upset person – your client.

ANALYZING YOUR OPTIONS

This method is explained in depth in the Workbook. It is also discussed in our book *It's All Your Fault at Work,* with several examples. Once again, this approach helps an upset client focus more on problem-solving for the future, rather than on blame and the past.

REMEMBER TO BREATHE

Advise clients about the benefits of breathing.

EXAMPLES OF UPSET EMOTIONS AND HOMEWORK

For this section, assist your client if there is time to discuss the scenarios at the end of Session 5. If there isn't time, just save this discussion for the next session.

PRACTICE CONVERSATION

If there's time, you can do a practice conversation with the client, to help prepare for dealing with a potentially difficult person in the coming week. Of course, you may be out of time or your client may not wish to do a practice exercise. It's just an option you can offer.

SESSION 5: MANAGED EMOTIONS: CALMING YOURSELF

REVIEWING HOMEWORK

First, review the homework from the last session with your coach.

Write something you learned from discussing your homework with your coach.

In this session we're going to look at ways that you can manage your own emotions:

Giving yourself an encouraging statement (Your "STAR")

Taking a break

Talking with someone who's not involved

Analyzing your options

MANAGED EMOTIONS

As we face new situations in this rapidly changing world, there are many times that we will feel upset. If you are going through a job change, a move, a divorce, or any other change, you know what we are talking about. You might feel confused, worried, angry, or sad. Yet upset feelings are just feelings and can be managed. Emotions are normal and we all have lots of them.

The goal isn't to eliminate feelings. The goal is to understand what we are feeling and to make decisions about which feelings to act on and which feelings to set aside; which feelings to show and which feelings to hide. Feelings are information which may help us, if we *think* before we act. But what do we do with the feelings that are so upsetting?

Before your meet with your coach, if possible, or with your coach:

Think of when your upset feelings got in the way of solving a problem, or created a problem:

Discuss this situation with your coach.

CALMING YOUR UPSET EMOTIONS

ENCOURAGING STATEMENTS

In Session 2 we briefly looked at how managed emotions can help someone through situations where unmanaged emotions would get them into trouble. One thing that helps is to give yourself encouraging statements. We call these your personal "STAR".

YOUR "STAR"

Your personal STAR stands for Statements That Are Reinforcing to you. Write up to three encouraging statements that you can use in a variety of difficult situations to reinforce yourself: Examples: "Easy does it." "This too shall pass." "One day at a time." "It's not about me."

_____

_____

_____

_____

TAKING A BREAK

One of the most successful ways of calming yourself enough to think clearly is to take a break. This can mean excusing yourself from an angry conversation for a few minutes. "Let me just stop and think for a few minutes." "Let's discuss this later." "I just need some time to think."

Before you meet with your coach, if possible, or with your coach:
Write down a situation when you took a break and it helped you calm down:

_____

_____

Write down a situation that might occur in the future, when you might need to take a break:

_____

_____

_____

Write down what you could say or do in the situation above, so that you could take a break:

_____

_____

Discuss these situations with your coach.

Practice saying you need a break with your coach playing someone in your life. Discuss how it felt to say that. Write it here:

_____

_____

_____

_____

_____

Another approach to taking a break is the "24 hour rule" before responding to a situation, such as by email, voicemail and so forth. Wait 24 hours before you send, call or do something else in response.

TALKING TO SOMEONE WHO IS NOT INVOLVED.

Work can be very upsetting at times. When we get upset, it often helps to talk to someone else about it. If possible, it is best to talk to someone who will stay out of the conflict and just lend an ear, so that they don't make things worse for you. Pick someone and call them or visit them and say: "I just need someone to listen for a few minutes. Are you available?"

Think of three people you could call when you are upset. Think of them as your **"Collective Wisdom Team"**:

_____

_____

_____

_____

_____

ANALYZING YOUR OPTIONS

When we're upset, it's easy to just focus on our feelings, which often keep us upset. Sometimes it helps to focus away from our feelings and onto solving a problem. One way of doing this is to write a list of options we have for solving a problem. While we're making our list, we start using a planning part of our brain that is calmer and more able to focus outward.

You can approach this process of analyzing options in three steps with your coach:

Brainstorm several possible options for yourself and write them down.

Check yourself for unrealistic options.

Select an option and analyze it carefully.

KEY QUESTIONS

When you are analyzing options, here are several key questions you can ask yourself:

Is this option realistic and practical to execute?

Will this option effectively resolve the problem or at least manage it successfully?

Does this option require the buy-in of anyone else and can I count on their assistance? Don't take their cooperation for granted. Check it out.

What are the pros and cons of this option? Be specific and ask yourself how important each of these pros and cons are to you. It may be helpful to rate each, with "3 = very important; 2 = somewhat important; or 1 = not important."

What are the most likely "What ifs" and how will I respond?

Is there anything else I must do or find out to ensure the success of this option?

What is the timetable and steps for each piece of the process?

How do my values and personal preferences align with this option?

Write a list here of options for addressing or solving a problem you are facing. This could be your Identified Problem or Issue from Session 1, or another problem. Don't analyze anything at first – just list a bunch of ideas without any criticism of them.

_____

_____

_____

_____

_____

_____

Now, focus on the most realistic options and analyze one of them by asking yourself the *Key Questions* above. Pick questions that seem the most helpful and write your responses next to the letter of the question (so you can look back and see what is was):

_____

_____

_____

_____

_____

_____

_____

Discuss with your coach how you answered those questions and see if you feel any less upset by talking about your options and analyzing them. Write something you learned from your discussion of this with your coach:

REMEMBER TO BREATHE

It's common knowledge that deep breathing helps to calm the nerves and center us. Take a few slow, deep breaths before responding to upsetting situations.

EXAMPLES OF UPSET EMOTIONS

Depending on the time available, discuss one or more of the following scenarios with your coach and then write down your responses.

HOMEWORK

If time is limited, then write your responses to the remaining scenarios as homework, to discuss with your coach at the beginning of Session 6:

1. Martha just found out that Jim is going to be an hour late to pick her up for a conference they are attending together. She is very upset as this will reduce the number of CEU Hours she was counting on for her professional certification. What could she do to calm her upset emotions?

Take a few deep breaths.

Repeat her STAR: There is a solution – I can find it!

Figure out how many CEUs she will now receive and determine where to make up the rest.

Speak empathically to Jim, whose car broke down and caused the delay.

2. Jack, in a phone conversation, threatened to take his chief vendor Hector to court over a minor contract dispute. What could Hector say to himself before he responds to Jack? How can Hector tell Jack he needs a break to calm down and sort things out?

Take a few deep breaths.

Repeat his STAR to himself: "I have confidence in my abilities."

Then, Hector could say to Jack: "I know this is very important to you and I want to call you back within the hour when I have all the documents and information in front of me."

3. Sarah comes into work and learns that her teammate has volunteered their services to coordinate the office holiday party without consulting with her. She is furious as she was planning a family vacation during that time period. What can she do to calm her emotions? What would be an example of flexible thinking to resolve this issue?

She can say to herself "This is not a 4-Alarm fire!"

She can tell her teammates that she is willing to help with preparations, but will continue with her vacation plans and not be there on the day of the event.

She can ask another workgroup to handle the holiday party in exchange for Sarah's commitment to organize the summer picnic.

4. LeRoy comes to work and discovers that his shift has been changed for the following month by the new supervisor without any consultation. LeRoy is enraged because this shift will make child –care arrangements extremely hard. What can LeRoy do to calm his emotions? How should he approach the new supervisor?

Take a few deep breaths.

Ask for an appointment with the new supervisor and explain his dilemma and ask for his help.

Approach his union rep to help him resolve this problem.

Propose a different work schedule to his supervisor that might also address the supervisor's needs (a win-win).

SESSION 6: MANAGED EMOTIONS: STAYING CALM AROUND OTHERS

COACHING TIPS

EMOTIONS ARE CONTAGIOUS

There is a lot that has been written about how emotions pass from one person to the next. Daniel Goleman writes a lot about this with emotional intelligence, first with his landmark book titled *Emotional Intelligence* and more recently with his book *Social Intelligence*. These are good references if you or your client want to look further into this topic.

What is interesting about all of this is that if someone is aware of the potential impact of others' emotions, one can avoid being as influenced by them. Helping your client become aware of this in his or her workplace will ease feelings of helplessness, as your client learns that he or she can avoid absorbing the emotions generated by others – especially the most difficult personalities around them.

NEGATIVE ADVOCATE

Building upon the theme of emotions being contagious, it's not hard to notice when others in the workplace start becoming "negative advocates" who pick up a fight without necessarily knowing much about it. They're just emotionally hooked, even though they are uninformed. You might ask your client if he or she knows anyone who tends to play such a role in other people's lives at work. Most of us know someone who does this a lot.

YOURSELF

When asking your client to remember scenarios of picking up others' emotions or pressuring others to have the same emotions as your client, make sure to point out that this is usually not a conscious activity. Most of the time, people pick up others' emotions without even realizing it. Then they tend to become defensive if you challenge them and say they were simply copying what someone else was doing. It's best to not confront such people with their negative behavior, but rather provide useful information.

Your client may feel defensive when asked about a time when he or she wanted others to feel the same way. People with personality problems may have a hard time recognizing that other people have other independent feelings which can be just as valid. This is one of the hardest things for high-conflict individuals, and some of your clients may have high-conflict patterns of behavior, although not all have personality disorders. So just be matter-of-fact about everyone seeking negative advocates at some time, especially when we are upset.

CALMING OTHER PEOPLE'S UPSET EMOTIONS

This section is excerpted from an article titled *Calming Upset People with EAR,* by Bill Eddy. A copy of the full article is in Appendix A of this Coaching Manual. If you find it helpful, you may make copies of this article and distribute it to any colleagues, clients or others you wish. You can also watch a pre-recorded Webinar video on this subject at www.HighConflictInstitute.com.

You are encouraged to read the article and/or watch the Webinar video for greater understanding of this method before doing the exercises with your client.

SESSION 6: MANAGED EMOTIONS: STAYING CALM AROUND OTHERS

Discuss with your coach your responses to the problem scenarios at the end of the last session. If you didn't write responses, you can read and discuss them now.

Write something you learned from discussing these examples with your coach:

Nothing is black or white – there may be options.

If I can remember to breathe, it's easier to think.

EMOTIONS ARE CONTAGIOUS

Emotions are contagious. Recent brain research has shown this. If someone is feeling happy, others around him or her will start to feel happier too. If someone is feeling sad, those nearby may also feel sad feelings. Sometimes people pressure us to have the same feeling they are having, especially when they are angry.

EXAMPLE

What do you think about this conversation?

Chuck: "Monty, do you know what Sally just did? She added her name to my report, before she handed it in. I can't believe she did that to me."

Monty: "Oh, I can't stand when people do that. She deserves to rot in hell! What kind of report was it?"

Chuck: "It was supposed to be a team report, but I did most of the work."

The next time Monty saw Sally in the hallway, he looked away and didn't even say "Hi."

Notice how Monty responded angrily without even knowing what kind of report it was. Did he "catch" the same feeling that Chuck had? Discuss it with your coach.

WOULD THIS BE A BETTER WAY TO RESPOND?

Chuck: "Monty, do you know what Sally just did? She added her name to my report, before she handed it in. I can't believe she did that to me."

Monty: "That sounds pretty frustrating. Is there anything for you to do about it now?"

Chuck: "No, I guess I just have to live with her sharing the credit."

Monty: "Oh well."

The next time Monty saw Sally in the hallway, he said "Hi" as he passed her.

Monty didn't seem to simply absorb the same emotions, but he still seemed to have some empathy for Chuck. He didn't seem to let it affect his relationship with Sally.

DON'T BE A NEGATIVE ADVOCATE

People become negative advocates for others when they absorb their emotions and just react the same way without thinking. People have different points of view, but this can get cloudy when someone is emotionally intense. The way to avoid becoming a negative advocate is to think for yourself, such as:

"What's my point of view about this situation?"

"Is this really a problem I need to get involved with?"

"Just because they are upset doesn't mean that I have to be upset or do anything differently."

Did Monty in the first situation above become a negative advocate for Chuck? Was he "negatively advocating" for Chuck by treating Sally the same way that Chuck would have, even though he didn't know much about the situation? A lot of conflicts get going in organizations when people advocate for others because they absorb the emotions and act on them, but are uninformed.

YOURSELF

Write a situation in which someone wanted you to feel the same way he or she felt:

A co-worker wanted me to get mad at our manager for changing our shift due to cross-training activities.

Describe to your coach how it felt to have someone pressure you to have the same feeling that they were having. Explain how you handled the situation. (Did you have the same feeling?) Write down how you would have preferred that the other person handled the situation.

I felt uncomfortable.

I felt differently, because I thought that cross-training was important so that we could learn each other's job responsibilities a little bit.

The other person could have expressed how he felt, but not have pushed me to also make a complaint.

Write a situation in which you pressured someone to feel the same as you felt (we all have):

I didn't want to take a business trip and I pressured my colleague into trying to talk the manager out of scheduling the trip.

Discuss with your coach why you wanted another person to feel the same way as you did. Did you want them to take your side, just to feel better? Discuss whether the person agreed with you or was able to have his or her own feelings about the situation. Discuss another way you could have dealt with the situation.

I wanted my colleague to take my side, because I didn't want to be viewed as the only one complaining about the trip. In retrospect, I should have respected my colleague's opinion that the trip was no big deal and I could have suggested that the colleague take the trip with another co-worker, which would have been acceptable to the manager.

Discuss with your coach how you can become aware sooner of picking up someone else's feelings, moods, or behaviors.

Think of two things you can tell yourself to help you avoid picking up other people's feelings without realizing it or becoming a negative advocate:

That is their feeling – what is mine?

Think about what is being said, – do I agree?

How can you protect others from your upset emotions during an angry or frustrating time at work? Describe how you might do this:

Take a break

Remove myself from the situation

24-hour rule

Remember to breathe

CALMING OTHER PEOPLE'S UPSET EMOTIONS

We can actually have a "contagious emotions" effect on other people in a positive way. If we can stay calm when others are upset, they will often calm down as well. The following is a good method of staying calming and potentially calming others. This is especially helpful if someone is upset with you – whether they are an employee, a supervisor or a customer!

E.A.R. STATEMENTS

E.A.R. stands for Empathy, Attention and Respect. It is the opposite of what you may feel like giving someone when he or she is upset – especially if they are attacking YOU! You'll be amazed at how effective this is at calming people down when you do it right.

An E.A.R. Statement connects with the person's experience, with their feelings. For example, let's say that someone verbally attacks you for not returning a phone call as quickly as he or she would have liked. "You don't respect me! You don't care how long I have to wait to deal with this problem! You're not doing your job!"

Rather than defending yourself, give the person an E.A.R. Statement, such as: "I can hear how upset you are. Tell me what's going on. I share your concerns about this problem and respect your efforts to solve it." This statement included:

EMPATHY: "I can hear how upset you are."

ATTENTION: "Tell me what's going on."

RESPECT: "I respect your efforts."

THE IMPORTANCE OF EMPATHY

Empathy is different from sympathy. Having empathy for someone means that you can feel the pain and frustration that they are feeling, and probably have felt similar feelings in your own life. These are normal human emotions and they are normally triggered in the people nearby. (Remember, emotions are contagious!) When you show empathy for another person, you are treating them as an equal who you are concerned about and can relate to their distress.

Sympathy is when you see someone else in a bad situation that you are not in. You may feel sorry for them and have sympathy for them, but it is a "one-up and one-down" position. There is more of a separation between those who give sympathy and those who receive it.

You don't have to use the word "empathy" to make a statement that shows empathy. For example:

"I can see how important this is to you."

"I understand this can be frustrating."

"I know this process can be confusing."

"I'm sorry to see that you're in this situation."

"I'd like to help you if I can."

"Let's see if we can solve this together."

"I'll work with you on this."

THE IMPORTANCE OF ATTENTION

There are many ways to let a person know that you will pay attention. For example, you can say:

"I will listen as carefully as I can."

"I will pay attention to your concerns."

"Tell me what's going on."

"Tell me more!"

You can also show attention non-verbally, such as:

Have good "eye contact" (keeping your eyes focused on the person)

Nod your head slowly up and down to show that you are attentive to their concerns

Lean in to pay closer attention

Put your hand near them, such as on the table beside them

(Be careful about touching an upset person – it may be misinterpreted as a threat, a come-on, or a put-down)

THE IMPORTANCE OF RESPECT

Anyone in distress needs respect from others. Even the most difficult and upset person usually has some quality that you can respect. By recognizing that quality, you can calm a person who is desperate to be respected. Here are several statements showing respect:

"I can see that you are a hard worker."

"I respect your commitment to solving this problem."

"I respect your efforts on this."

"I respect your success at accomplishing that other task."

"You have important skills that we need here."

MANAGE YOUR AMYGDALA

We are very sensitive to other's emotions, especially threats, because they trigger the amygdala in our brains. We have one in the middle of our right hemisphere of our brains and one in the middle of our left. Of course, if someone is real upset with us, giving an EAR Statement is the opposite of what we feel like doing. But it will help you a lot if you can calm them down – and this method works much better than telling someone: "Calm down!!" That usually makes them more upset, because your tone of voice triggers their amygdala.

IT'S NOT ABOUT YOU!

If someone is intensely upset with you, remind yourself it's not about you! Don't take it personally. It's about the person's own upset and lack of sufficient skills to manage his or her own emotions. Intense upsets are inappropriate in today's work world, where we need to use our calm logic as much as possible, rather than just reacting to things.

Try making E.A.R. statements and you will find they often end any personal attack and calm the person down. This is especially true for high conflict people (HCPs) who regularly have a hard time calming themselves down.

Empathy, Attention, and Respect can be calming, because they let the person know that you want to connect with him or her, rather than threaten him or her.

Making E.A.R. statements – or non-verbally showing your Empathy, Attention, and Respect – may help you avoid many potentially difficult situations. It can save you time, money and emotional energy for years to come.

Think of an EAR Statement you might use with someone at work who gets upset sometimes. Write it down here. It doesn't have to be long. It can just include some words that show Empathy, or Attention, or Respect, or all three:

I know you are under a lot of pressure and you're committed to doing the best job that you can. Please let me know how I can help.

With your coach practice a conversation in which you give an EAR Statement to a person who is upset about somebody else – possibly in the coming week.

Then, practice a conversation in which you give an EAR statement to someone who is upset with you.

Write down something you learned from this exercise with your coach:

EAR statements will calm people down.

Sometimes giving EAR statements is the opposite of what we feel.

SESSION 7: MODERATE BEHAVIOR: BIFF RESPONSES TO HOSTILE EMAIL

COACHING TIPS

BIFF RESPONSES TO HOSTILE EMAIL

Encourage your client to write a BIFF response to the refrigerator example in this section before turning the page and looking at the sample answer. We left this answer in the Workbook to help the client see what a BIFF Response could look like.

NO ONE RIGHT WAY

The ten questions contained in this section are drawn from an article titled *Coaching For BIFF Responses*, which is contained in Appendix B of this Manual. You are encouraged to read that before doing the discussion and exercise of Annie and George Brown. It will help you explain the ten questions you are asking your client.

It is especially important to ask all ten questions before giving any of your own input into how a BIFF Response should be written. One of the common errors professionals make is to tell their clients how to do things, rather than helping their client learn how to do them so that they can do them on their own. Learning how to write BIFF Responses is a very empowering experience. Clients usually feel proud of what they have written and often start using BIFF Responses right away on the same day that they have learned how to do them.

For more information about BIFF Responses, see the book *BIFF: Quick Responses to High-Conflict people* by Bill Eddy, and/or watch the Webinar titled *Coaching for BIFF Responses*. There is also a video available for clients titled: *How to Write a BIFF Response*.

We have taught so many people this method since 2007, that we are now hearing of clients who learned to write BIFF responses to angry people in their lives and now the angry people are writing back using the same BIFF format, without having been taught the method! It just looks good and feels good to write email and letter responses that are civil and assertive, without attacking or being rude back.

SESSION 7: MODERATE BEHAVIOR: BIFF RESPONSES TO HOSTILE EMAIL

One area of modern life that frustrates almost everyone is angry email correspondence. One method of responding to hostile emails in a *moderate way* is to write them as BIFF Responses: Brief, Informative, Friendly and Firm (BIFF).

BUT FIRST, DO YOU NEED TO RESPOND?

Much of hostile mail or email does not need a response. Email from irritating co-workers, (ex-) spouses, angry neighbors or even attorneys do not usually have legal significance. The email itself has no power, unless you give it power. Often, it is emotional venting aimed at relieving the writer's anxiety. If you respond with similar emotions and hostility, you will simply escalate things without satisfaction, and just get a new piece of hostile mail back. In most cases, you are better off not responding.

However, some letters and emails develop power when copies are filed in a complaint process – or get sent to other important people in your life. In these cases, it may be important to respond to inaccurate statements with accurate statements of fact. If you need to respond, we recommend a BIFF Response™: Be Brief, Informative, Friendly and Firm.

BRIEF

Keep your response brief. This will reduce the chances of a prolonged and angry back and forth. The more you write, the more material the other person has to criticize. Keeping it brief signals that you don't wish to get into a dialogue. Just make your response and end your letter. Don't take their statements personally and don't respond with a personal attack. Avoid focusing on comments about the person's character, such as saying he or she is rude, insensitive, or stupid. It just escalates the conflict and keeps it going. You don't have to defend yourself to someone you disagree with. If your friends still like you, you don't have to prove anything to those who don't.

INFORMATIVE

The main reason to respond to hostile mail is to correct inaccurate statements which might be seen by others. "Just the facts" is a good idea. Focus on the accurate statements you want to make, not on the inaccurate statements the other person made. For example: "Just to clear things up, I was out of town on February 12th, so I would not have been the person who was making loud noises that day."

Avoid negative comments. Avoid sarcasm. Avoid threats. Avoid personal remarks about the other's intelligence, ethics, or moral behavior. If the other person is angry, you will have no success in reducing the conflict with personal attacks. While most people can ignore personal attacks or might think harder about what you are saying, high conflict people feel they have no choice but to respond in anger – and keep the conflict going. Personal attacks rarely lead to insight or positive change.

FRIENDLY

While you may be tempted to write in anger, you are more likely to achieve your goals by writing in a friendly manner. A friendly response will increase your chances of getting a friendly – or neutral – response in return. If your goal is to end the conflict, then add a friendly greeting and friendly closing. Don't give the other person a reason to get defensive and keep responding. Make it sound as relaxed and non-antagonistic as possible. Brief comments that show your empathy and respect will generally calm the other person down, even if only for a short time.

FIRM

In a non-threatening way, tell the other person your information or concerns about an issue. (For example: "That's all I'm going to say on this issue.") Be careful not to make comments that invite more discussion, such as: "I hope you will agree with me …." This invites the other person to tell you "I *don't agree.*" Just give your friendly closing and then stop.

However, if you need a decision from the other person, then end with two choices, such as: "Please let me know by Friday at 5pm if I should pick up those documents or you will send them to me." By limiting it to two choices, you are less likely to trigger a new argument. By giving a response date and time, you avoid having to keep contacting the person. If he or she does not respond by then, you can choose whether to ask again or take other action.

Firm doesn't mean harsh. Just sound confident and end the back-and-forth nature of hostile communications. A confident-sounding person is less likely to be challenged with further emails. If you get further emails, you can ignore them, if you have already sufficiently addressed the inaccurate information. If you need to respond again, keep it even briefer and do not emotionally engage. In fact, it often helps to just repeat the key information using the same words.

EXAMPLE: PATTY'S REFRIGERATOR

You're going to have a chance to write a BIFF Response to Patty's situation. Patty's refrigerator has stopped working – one day after her warranty ran out. One month after she bought the refrigerator, she was given the opportunity to buy an extended warranty for 2-3 years for $50, beyond the initial 1 year warranty that came with the refrigerator. She's furious and has written the following email to the company.

> Dear Sirs:
>
> Just over a year ago I purchased one of your refrigerators. But it stopped working 1 year AND 1 DAY later!!! I was told that it came with a one year warranty and that your company would not pay for the repairs, since I did not get the additional repair insurance beyond the first year.
>
> I AM CERTAIN THAT YOU KNEW THAT IT WOULD FAIL! This is irresponsible and insulting to me as a customer. I am telling everyone how irresponsible and unethical your company is.
>
> I demand that you pay for my repairs. I have attached a copy of the bill I paid for $195 to fix the part that failed so quickly. YOU MUST MAKE THIS RIGHT!!!
>
> Sincerely,
> Ms. Patty Jones

First, look at the following response and write down ways in which it is probably not a "BIFF Response."

SAMPLE RESPONSE #1:

> Dear Ms. Jones:
>
> I'm sorry to see that you are in this situation. Unfortunately, it's your own fault that you didn't get the extra insurance to cover your refrigerator repairs. Since it was your error and not ours that you didn't get the insurance coverage, we will not be compensating you for your repairs. I guess you've learned your lesson now. We have great products, so I recommend against spreading rumors that we are not a good company or you could face strong action from us.
> Good Luck!   Mary, Your Customer Service Rep

Write down ways in which the above response is not a "BIFF Response."

Blame – that it's her fault for not getting insurance

Admonishment – "you learned your lesson."

Threats – to take legal action

Now, write your own response as Mary, the Customer Service representative, which is Brief, Informative, Friendly and Firm (B.I.F.F. Response) to Patty Jones.

_____

_____

_____

_____

_____

_____

_____

_____

_____

_____

Discuss your response with your Coach, who will ask you several questions about your response to help you think about it.

Then, review the following response. Would this be a good BIFF Response?

SAMPLE RESPONSE #2:

Dear Ms. Jones:

Thank you for writing to us about your refrigerator. I was saddened to hear about your problem with it. Unfortunately, the company has a strict policy which prevents us from extending the 1-year warranty, even one day (even though I wish I could). However, I am authorized to give you a credit coupon toward this repair or a future purchase worth $50, if you would like me to do so, for your effort in taking the time to write us. Let me know if you would like that and I will send it to you. I wish you all the best in the coming year.

Take care, Mary, the Customer Service Rep

Do you think this is a BIFF Response? Write why or why not here:

_____

_____

_____

_____

NO ONE RIGHT WAY

There's no one right way to write a BIFF Response. What's important is that it is Brief, Informative, Friendly, and Firm. Two people could write two good BIFF Responses to the same situation that are different, based on 3 key factors:

Who the BIFF writer is.

Who the BIFF reader is.

What the situation is.

So the above **Sample Response #2** might be a good BIFF Response and your response on the previous page might be a good BIFF Response, even if they are different.

YOURSELF

Think of an email that you received recently or use the following example. Practice writing a BIFF Response to that email.

> Dear Mr. Brown,
>
> _I demand to know why you are suddenly making arrangements for the annual dinner! That has been my responsibility for the past three years, and you know it. This is an insult to me and to our company. You have no respect for anyone else's job. How would you like it if I came to your office and organized a party and didn't invite you! So stop talking to the caterer – that you have chosen without consulting with anyone – and let me organize the annual dinner! You are a rude and selfish person, who just wants to get credit and attention for organizing this. Just get out of the way!_
>
> _Annie_

Suppose that Annie was out sick for a couple days and you, as George Brown, thought she wasn't going to want to do it. He thought he was doing her a favor to volunteer to do this. Write your response as Mr. Brown without getting defensive. Remember: Brief, Informative, Friendly and Firm.

Your BIFF Response (as George Brown):

> _Dear Annie,_
> _Unfortunately, I assumed that you would want help with this project since you were out sick. I should have checked with you and not taken this over. I will forward my notes immediately and would be happy to help in any way you would desire._
> _Sincerely,_
> _George_

Now, ask yourself several questions about it, then discuss with your coach.

Is it Brief?

Is it Informative?

Is it Friendly?

Is it Firm?

Does it contain any Advice?

Does it contain any Admonishments?

Does it contain any Apologies?

How do you think the other person will respond?

Is there anything you would take out, add or change?

Would you like to hear my thoughts about it?

Now, discuss it with your coach. Write down something you learned:

BIFF responses can be brief.

I learned that we should always check our assumptions before acting.

CONCLUSION

Whether you are at work, at home or elsewhere, a BIFF Response is an easy way to save yourself time and emotional anguish when you respond, while you look good to your co-workers and supervisors. It's a *moderate behavior* in response to an extreme behavior. The more people who handle hostile email in this manner, the less hostile email there will be.

SESSION 8: MODERATE BEHAVIOR: AVOIDING EXTREME BEHAVIORS

COACHING TIPS

FOUR SCENARIOS

Help your client analyze the four scenarios provided, in terms of extreme behavior and moderate behavior.

You can also suggest that you have a practice conversation for one or more of the exercise scenarios, to strengthen your client's ability to respond moderately in a lively conversation.

HOMEWORK: A FULL METHOD EXAMPLE

At the end of this chapter there is a homework assignment applying a workplace scenario to the full method taught in the Workbook. Following the assignment there is a full sample answer to assist in your discussion – whether at the end of Session 8 or at the beginning of Session 9.

SESSION 8: MODERATE BEHAVIOR: AVOIDING EXTREME BEHAVIORS

We'll start this session reviewing how you can use moderate behavior in dealing with the following situations. Then we'll give you a chance to come up with some situations of your own. Write responses to the following scenarios, to discuss with your coach:

THE SHARED OFFICE

1. Beth learns that she will have to give up her private office that she loves and has had for several years due to a facility downsizing. She has been paired to share an office with another employee, April, who is a nice person but on the opposite end of the political spectrum. This individual has talk radio playing in her office constantly.

Describe an extreme behavior Beth could demonstrate in response to this situation.

Pull the plug from the radio and say "Enough!"

Describe a moderate behavior that Beth could demonstrate in response to this situation.

Propose to her office mate that they both wear earphones so that they can listen to different radio stations at the same time.

Looking forward, which behavioral response has the best chance of facilitating a decent working relationship and a resolution to the talk radio issue?

The moderate behavior has the best chance, because the proposal could be done by both parties.

Discuss with your coach.

Write something you learned from your discussion with your coach about this scenario:

That a proposal can solve a lot of potential conflicts.

THE COLD MANAGER

2. Nancy is a manager who must work closely with Diane, the manager of another department. Despite Nancy's efforts at pleasantries this individual is remote, cold and answers the phone (after hearing who it is) in the most unfriendly manner. She does however, provide important information. Nancy tries to prepare herself prior to calling Diane but admits that this behavior is really getting to her.

What could Nancy do that would be regarded as extreme behavior in response to Diane?

Confront Diane and tell her to stop being such a jerk when she answers the phone.

What could Nancy do that would be considered a moderate behavior?

Thank Diane for answering the phone and get to the point. End the conversation with "Thank you for your help."

After hanging up the phone, immediately tell herself her STAR.

Looking forward, which behavior has the chance of facilitating a decent working relationship?

The moderate behavior will keep the information flowing.

Discuss with your coach.

Write something you learned from your discussion with your coach about this scenario:

A STAR can be reinforcing when a situation feels like a put-down.

THE RESTAURANT KITCHEN

3. Andy works in a restaurant kitchen. The chef, Carlos, has frequent tirades and has been known to throw objects when enraged. Andy feels this behavior is insulting and uncalled for. Andy has reached his limit with the bullying.

What behavioral response would be extreme for Andy?

To throw something back at the chef

To abruptly quit

What behavioral response would be moderate for Andy?

He could say: "Sorry you're having a bad day, Chef. But do not yell at me – it doesn't help."

"Easy does it, Chef. Yelling doesn't fix anything."

Which behavior has the better chance of establishing a decent working relationship and limit setting on the bullying behavior?

The moderate behavior, because it responds to the bullying behavior in a constructive way

Discuss with your coach.

Write something you learned from your discussion with your coach about this scenario:

You CAN set limits with bullies

THE ADMINISTRATIVE ASSISTANT

4. Jean works as an administrative assistance to Ted. She describes him as a friendly high energy person and for the most part enjoys working for him. Ted however has the habit of dropping work off to Jean in the last hour of the work day and expecting it to be on his desk by early morning. This issue has stressed Jean out considerably. She is angry at his insensitivity. She has had to miss dinner with her family or leave home earlier than necessary to accommodate him on numerous occasions.

What behavioral response would be extreme for Jean?

To abruptly quit

To refuse to work

What behavioral response would be moderate?

To explain to her boss that she wants to help and that any work he needs by the following morning needs to be on her desk by 4pm.

Which behavioral response has the better chance of establishing a decent working relationship and the resolution of this issue?

The moderate, because she won't quit

Discuss with your coach.

Write something you learned from your discussion with your coach about this scenario:

I learned to reinforce setting limits

Now, think of a situation related to your Identified Problem or Issue where you may have engaged in extreme behavior. **Write down** what you could do in the future if faced with the same situation using a moderate behavior instead:

Discuss with your coach. Write down something you learned from the discussion:

_____

_____

_____

_____

_____

_____

_____

_____

HOMEWORK: A FULL METHOD EXAMPLE

If time permits, read the following exercise and answer the questions for Debbie, given what you know from the below information and what you imagine her issues are. If there isn't time to answer the questions during this session, write it as homework and bring it to the next Session 9. You can look ahead at Session 9 for explanations of some of the questions involved in this example.

THE MEDICAL RECEPTIONIST

Debbie gets a new job as a medical receptionist. She is very excited to obtain employment so close to her home and with such a reputable medical group.

However, within days Debbie recognizes that the Office Manager, Jill, "has problems." One minute she is friendly enough. The next minute she doesn't respond or cuts off the conversation. The other women in the office confide that two previous receptionists quite because of Jill. According to these women, Jill has been raising her young active grandchildren as her daughter is incarcerated on drug charges. Apparently Jill is also unhappily married.

Debbie feels empathy for Jill upon hearing this information, however, as the weeks pass, Jill's behavior continues to be provocative and demeaning. Debbie seeks counseling to decide what to do.

She meets with a counselor and discussed the "Jill problem." After explaining the situation, they begin to use the _New Ways for Work_ method.

Identified Problem. Write a statement here summarizing Debbie's problem:

_____

_____

_____

FLEXIBLE THINKING

Think Check. Write what Debbie might say to herself regarding the situation:

Is my thinking "all-or-nothing"? _____

_____

Am I using emotional reasoning? _____

_____

Am I minimizing the positive or maximizing the negative? _____

_____

Am I using overgeneralizations? _____

_____

Am I personalizing anything? _____

_____

Am I making any assumptions? _____

_____

Analyzing Options. Write what Debbie might see as some options for herself:

_____

_____

_____

_____

_____

_____

Making Proposals. Write two proposals that Debbie could make to her boss:

_____

_____

_____

_____

MANAGED EMOTIONS

Emotion Check. Write what Debbie might say about her own emotions:

Did I raise my voice? _____

_____

Did I yell or scream? _____

_____

Did I threaten anything? _____

_____

Did I say regrettable things? _____

_____

Did I upset the other person? _____

_____

Did my anger get in the way of my message? _____

_____

Calming others with E.A.R. Write ways Debbie might calm her boss:

_____

_____

_____

WORKBOOK - PAGE 49

Create some STARs (Statements That Are Reinforcing) for Debbie:

_____

_____

_____

_____

MODERATE BEHAVIOR

Behavior Check. Write what Debbie might say about her own behavior:

Did I insult anyone? _____

_____

Was I rude or inappropriate? _____

_____

Was my behavior aggressive? _____

_____

Did I go against any work policies? (Late, missed meetings, missed deadlines, absences, etc.)

_____

_____

Did my behavior put myself or others at risk? _____

_____

Could I have substituted a moderate behavior? _____

_____

New behavior goal at work. Write a new goal for Debbie:

_____

_____

_____

_____

Practicing new behaviors. Write what Debbie can practice to get to her goal:

_____

_____

_____

_____

_____

Discuss your answers with your coach at the end of this session or the beginning of Session 9.

Write something that you have learned from doing this exercise:

_____

_____

_____

_____

_____

SAMPLE ANSWER – FOR COACH (NOT IN WORKBOOK)

The following is a sample answer you can discuss with your client, after first hearing what your client has written. This will probably be discussed at the beginning of Session 9, as it is homework at the end of Session 8. This is how Debbie's writing and discussions might have gone with her counselor:

Identified Problem. Write a statement here summarizing Debbie's problem:

The Office Manager at my job treats me disrespectfully and makes it very difficult to work together.

FLEXIBLE THINKING

Think Check. Write what Debbie might say to herself regarding the situation:

Is my thinking "all-or-nothing"?

No, I see her positive qualities as well. But sometimes I think I'm just going to quit – but that would be all-or-nothing.

Am I using emotional reasoning?

I'm trying not to over-react to her.

Am I minimizing the positive or maximizing the negative?

I don't think so, but I'll discuss with my counselor to see if I'm missing something.

Am I using overgeneralizations?

I'm trying not to see her as all bad.

Am I personalizing anything?

I'm trying to see that it's about her and not about me.

Analyzing Options. Write what Debbie might see as some options for her:

I should find another job.

I could do nothing.

I could complain to the head doctor.

In her discussions with her counselor, here's what she might have said about these options:

Beginning to look for another job appeals to me. I don't want to be put in the position of abruptly quitting.

I recognize that I can't do this for long, as "disrespect" is a trigger for me.

I want to rule out complaining to the head doctor, because the Office Manager has been there for 15 years and I don't think that will help.

Suppose, after careful consideration, Debbie decides to actively look for another job, while trying to cope with the situation until that time.

Making Proposals. Write two proposals that Debbie could make to her boss:

Debbie realizes that it would be easier to look for a new job if she has time to interview. Since the office has been slow without much for her to do, she proposes the following:

I suggest that I reduce my hours by 4-8 hours per week, depending on how business is going.

Since we tend to be slow mid-week, I propose that I specifically take off Wednesdays all day or work a half-day.

Suppose that the Office Manager says "Yes," to her proposals, and that it will be the afternoon or full day, depending on the amount of work. She will let Debbie know on Mondays each week. This way, Debbie has time for job interviews on Wednesday afternoons and possibly Wednesday mornings.

MANAGED EMOTIONS

Emotion Check. Write what Debbie might say about her own emotions:

Did I raise my voice?

No. I stayed calm.

Did I yell or scream?

No.

Did I threaten anything?

No.

Did I say regrettable things?

No.

Did I upset the other person?

No, because I was careful and managed my emotions while I made my proposals.

Did my anger get in the way of my message?

No, because I was prepared and practiced with my counselor.

Calming others with E.A.R. Write how Debbie might calm her boss:

From time to time I can pay attention to her, ask how her weekend was and otherwise try to act friendly and respectful.

When she cuts me off rudely, I can just look unaffected and stay calm, rather than looking angry. So she won't have to get more defensive.

When the Office Manager is talking I can try to listen with empathy, even when it's issues that have nothing to do with work. While this won't change her erratic behavior, it may improve our interactions at the moment.

Create a couple STARs (Statements That Are Reinforcing) for Debbie:

This is only temporary.

I'm not the one with the problem.

MODERATE BEHAVIOR

Behavior Check. Write what Debbie might say about her own behavior:

Did I insult anyone?

No.

Was I rude or inappropriate?

No.

Was my behavior aggressive?

No. I'm careful to show empathy instead.

Did I go against any work policies? (Late, missed meetings, missed deadlines, absences, etc.)

No – although I felt like it!

Did my behavior put myself or others at risk?

No.

Could I have substituted a moderate behavior?

I think I am doing that.

New behavior goal at work. Write a new goal for Debbie:

When faced with the Office Manager's negativity, I want to respond in a way that manages the situation without making it worse.

Practicing new behaviors. Write what Debbie can practice to get to her goal:

I can ignore the negative behavior and just say "You seem stressed."

I can suggest "Perhaps we should discuss this at another time."

I could also say: "Ouch, that hurt." But that really depends on how she's treating me. I don't want to make myself more vulnerable to her.

Conclusion

Debbie was able to secure a new position in a medical office not far away. She is considerably happier and finds her new work group supportive and easier to work with.

By following the *New Ways for Work* method, Debbie was able to cope with the situation at the previous job, while looking for a new opportunity. She did not have to quit to deal with the situation, which would have created a serious financial burden.

SESSION 9: CHECKING YOURSELF

COACHING TIPS

HOMEWORK

Review your client's answer to the Medical Receptionist full method analysis from the end of Session 8.

THINK CHECK, EMOTION CHECK, AND BEHAVIOR CHECK

This chapter involves "checking yourself" for the client, to see if he or she can reflect on their thinking, emotions and behavior. The items to assist in checking are self-explanatory.

CHECKING YOURSELF FOR ALL THE SKILLS

These scenarios will assist your client in applying all of the new ways skills which have been discussed in this workbook. It is a good review and will help you make suggestions of what the client can work on in the future.

As with the other sessions, offer to do a practice conversation with the client for any of these scenarios.

DEVELOPING YOUR PLAN

This exercise helps the client to think ahead about when to check himself or herself. It's often helpful to do this in the morning before work – or whenever the client goes to work. It can also help to do this check before a particularly difficult meeting, as a reminder of how the client can manage himself or herself through it.

REVIEW OF MY GOALS

This provides the client with an opportunity to reflect on his or her original goals from Session 3, which can help in planning for the future. The client may decide to continue working on the same goals or may update them, for his or her own future growth.

This review of goals can also provide a sense of completion for working through all nine sessions of the Workbook and accomplishing some or all of these personal goals.

SESSION 9: CHECKING YOURSELF

Now, let's put it all together!

"Checking yourself" means making sure you're aware of using all the skills:

Flexible Thinking

Managed Emotions

Moderate Behaviors

THINK CHECK

First, we're going to focus on how to check your thinking. There are a few ways in which our thinking loses its flexibility. It can help to "check yourself" to see if you are using any of the following – what some people call "cognitive distortions" or negative thoughts that are inappropriate to the situation. Here's a simple guide you can use with your coach*:

#1 ALL OR NOTHING THINKING   YES OR NO

Seeing things in absolutes. Something is wonderful – or terrible.

#2 EMOTIONAL REASONING   YES OR NO

Assuming facts from how you feel "I feel stupid, therefore I am stupid".

#3 MINIMIZING THE POSITIVE/ MAXIMIZING THE NEGATIVE   YES OR NO

Distorting reality will keep you stuck and make you feel like a victim.

#4 OVERGENERALIZATIONS   YES OR NO

Drawing huge unproven conclusions from minor or rare events.

#5 PERSONALIZATION   YES OR NO

Taking personally unrelated events or events beyond your control.

#6 MAKING ASSUMPTIONS   YES OR NO

Assuming outcomes based on little information.

---

*Drawn from Bill Eddy's book *High Conflict People in Legal Disputes* (32), which refers to David D. Burns' book *The Feeling Good Handbook* (8-10).

EMOTION CHECK

When you are reacting to a situation or issue, be conscious of your emotional responses. It takes practice to monitor and adjust emotions. Use the following guide to check your emotions.

#1 Did I raise my voice?   YES OR NO

#2 Did I yell or scream?   YES OR NO

#3 Did I threaten anything?   YES OR NO

#4 Did I say regrettable things?   YES OR NO

#5 Did I upset the other person?   YES OR NO

#6 Did my anger get in the way of my message?   YES OR NO

If you notice a pattern of one of more of the above occurring, then discuss ways of changing those patterns with your coach.

BEHAVIOR CHECK

Review the following inappropriate behaviors in the workplace. It is very important to moderate your behavior, despite feeling anger or other high-intensity emotions. Use the following guide to check your own behavior.

#1 Did I insult anyone?   YES OR NO

#2 Was I rude or inappropriate?   YES OR NO

#3 Was my behavior aggressive?   YES OR NO

#4 Did I engage in behavior that is against work policy?   YES OR NO
(Late for work, missed meetings, missed deadlines, etc.)

#5 Did my behavior put myself or others at risk?   YES OR NO

#6 Could I have substituted a moderate behavior?   YES OR NO

CHECKING YOURSELF FOR ALL THE SKILLS

Now, read the following stories and determine if the problem is *all-or-nothing thinking, unmanaged emotions,* or *extreme behavior.* Then, describe what a more positive response could be.

Steve is putting in long days to finish an important work project. His assistant brings him the wrong set of documents and he flies into a rage, screaming at the assistant, swearing at the company and throwing the documents across the room.

Steve appears to be having a problem with

extreme behavior.

What's a "STAR" statement Steve could use to calm himself?

"No deadline is worth my integrity."

What could Steve do to handle the problem more effectively?

Leave work, rest and return in the morning.

What could Steve do to avoid the problem in the future?

Reorganize priorities and speak with his boss about realistic time tables.

How should Steve respond to the assistant he just screamed at?

He should apologize to the assistant and take responsibility.

If the assistant thinks Steve is a bully, would she be correct?

Yes!

What would be appropriate for the assistant to say to Steve in regards to his behavior, after the situation calmed down?

I appreciate your stress, but do not yell at me. It only makes everything worse.

If Steve regularly "checks himself" by asking himself if he's using the three skills above, do you think that would help him avoid flying into a rage and throwing documents?

Yes!

When should he check himself to avoid this occurring again?

Every few hours.

Joanne has been assigned for the third time to clean out the staff refrigerator. It is disgusting. Items have spilled and food is rotting. Joanne is becoming increasingly upset as she says to herself: "Why am I the company slave? Why do I always get this horrible job?"

Joanne is having a problem with?

All-or-nothing thinking.

What could Joanne do to handle the problem more effectively?

Offer a proposal about cleaning the refrigerator to her supervisor.

What could Joanne do to minimize the problem in the future?

Negotiate an acceptable proposal.

What "STAR" statement could Joanne use to help her get through the situation?

I will do my fair share.

Think of a proposal that Joanne could make to her supervisor about this:

That the refrigerator cleanup rotate among all the staff members and that everyone does it twice a month.

If Joanne regularly "checks herself" by asking herself if she's using the three skills above, do you think that would help her avoid becoming so upset about the refrigerator?

Yes

When should she check herself to avoid getting so upset?

Before going to work on her assigned cleanup days.

Carol has been assigned a new supervisor and she feels she just: "Can't get it right." The supervisor has become increasingly dissatisfied and Carol goes home every night with her stomach in knots. She is having trouble sleeping and keeps running the day's events over in her mind. She is feeling hopeless and depressed. As soon as she walks into the office, she feels scared and anxious.

Carol is having a problem with?

Unmanaged emotions.

What STAR Statement could Carol use to support herself?

This is not about me.

What could Carol do to handle the problem more effectively?

Speak to a counselor.

Who could Carol talk to? Why would it be helpful?

To her EAP or outside counselor for ways to handle problems when they arise.

DEVELOPING YOUR PLAN:

As this may be your last coaching session, discuss with your coach how you can address new situations, especially like the one that brought you to this coaching, so that you know how you can deal with it well in the future:

How and when will I regularly "check myself" for:

Flexible thinking:

_____

_____

Managed emotions:

_____

_____

Moderate behaviors:

_____

_____

_____

REVIEW OF MY GOALS:

As you finish, review your goals from Session 3 and what you have learned:

To use flexible thinking in dealing with difficult situations.

My personal goal:

_____

_____

What I have learned:

_____

_____

_____

TO MANAGE MY UPSET EMOTIONS DURING DIFFICULT SITUATIONS.

My personal goal:

_____

What I have learned:

_____

_____

TO USE MODERATE BEHAVIORS WITH OTHER EMPLOYEES, MANAGERS, AND CLIENTS/CUSTOMERS.

My personal goal:

_____

_____

What I have learned:

_____

_____

TO VALIDATE MY OWN STRENGTHS AND PERSONAL QUALITIES.

My personal goal:

_____

_____

What I have learned:

_____

_____

Congratulations! You have completed 9 sessions of *New Ways for Work!*

ADDITIONAL SESSIONS: CONTINUING TO CHECK MYSELF

COACHING TIPS

If you have more sessions available, such as a total of 12 sessions, you could use the last three sessions for monthly follow-up reviews. The form for "Continuing to Check Myself" is self-explanatory. You can have the client guide much of these sessions by describing their self-checking process. While the form emphasizes describing how a situation was handled successfully using the client's skills, each form ends with "Something I want to work on."

FUTURE SESSIONS

In some cases, you may have unlimited sessions with a client who wants to keep working with you. This is fine and you can continue to refer back to the self-checking process from time to time to reinforce it and help the client continue to grow in the use of his or her skills.

ADDITIONAL SESSIONS: CONTINUING TO CHECK MYSELF

You can use the following format to check the use of your skills each week, month or whatever period you check in with your coach to discuss the use of your skills.

An incident in which I used my skills to handle the situation better than in the past:

_____

_____

How did I succeed at using my improved skills? _____

_____

_____

FLEXIBLE THINKING:

Avoiding all-or-nothing thinking? _____

_____

_____

Making a proposal? _____

_____

_____

MANAGED EMOTIONS:

Remembering to breathe? _____

_____

_____

Giving myself an encouraging statement? _____

_____

_____

Taking a break? _____

_____

_____

Talking to someone uninvolved? _____

_____

Analyzing my options? _____

_____

Giving EAR Statements? _____

_____

_____

MODERATING MY BEHAVIOR:

Using BIFF Responses? _____

_____

_____

Avoiding extreme behaviors? _____

_____

_____

CHECKING MYSELF:

Regularly checking my use of my new skills? _____

_____

_____

Something I want to work on: _____

_____

_____

CONTINUING TO CHECK MYSELF

You can use the following format to check the use of your skills each week, month or whatever period you check in with your coach to discuss the use of your skills.

An incident in which I used my skills to handle the situation better than in the past:

_____

_____

How did I succeed at using my improved skills? _____

_____

FLEXIBLE THINKING:

Avoiding all-or-nothing thinking? _____

_____

Making a proposal? _____
_____

MANAGED EMOTIONS:

Remembering to breathe? _____
_____

Giving myself an encouraging statement? _____
_____

Taking a break? _____
_____

Talking to someone uninvolved? _____
_____

Analyzing my options? _____
_____

Giving EAR Statements? _____
_____

MODERATING MY BEHAVIOR:

Using BIFF Responses? _____
_____

Avoiding extreme behaviors? _____
_____
_____

CHECKING MYSELF:

Regularly checking my use of my new skills? _____

_____

_____

Something I want to work on: _____

_____

_____

CONTINUING TO CHECK MYSELF

You can use the following format to check the use of your skills each week, month or whatever period you check in with your coach to discuss the use of your skills.

An incident in which I used my skills to handle the situation better than in the past:

_____

_____

_____

How did I succeed at using improved skills? _____

_____

_____

FLEXIBLE THINKING:

Avoiding all-or-nothing thinking? _____

_____

_____

Making a proposal? _____

_____

_____

MANAGED EMOTIONS:

Remembering to breathe? _____

_____

_____

Giving myself an encouraging statement? _____

_____

Taking a break? _____

_____

Talking to someone uninvolved? _____

_____

Analyzing my options? _____

_____

_____

Giving EAR Statements? _____

_____

MODERATING MY BEHAVIOR:

Using BIFF Responses? _____

_____

Avoiding extreme behaviors? _____

_____

_____

CHECKING MYSELF:

Regularly checking my use of my new skills? _____

_____

_____

Something I want to work on: _____

_____

_____

WORKSHEETS

COACHING TIPS

The two worksheets at the end of the Workbook can be used by the client at any time in the future to help himself or herself to continue using and strengthening the four New Ways skills. They are self-explanatory, as follows.

WORKSHEETS

The following two worksheets can be used on a regular basis, if you wish, for checking yourself as you face and deal with problems and issues at work.

FULL METHOD FORMAT – EXERCISE WORKSHEET

For facing a problem situation:

This worksheet is designed to help you look at how to deal with an existing or upcoming situation at work. It focuses on what you have done in the situation so far (checking your thinking, emotions and behavior), and then what you can do going forward (looking at your options, making proposals to managers and goals for your own behavior).

CHECK YOURSELF – CHECKLIST

For looking back on a problem situation:

This is a handy short checklist for use in the middle of a problem or looking back on a problem.

FULL METHOD FORMAT – EXERCISE WORKSHEET

Identified Problem:

Write a statement here summarizing the problem:

_____

_____

_____

_____

_____

_____

FLEXIBLE THINKING

Think Check:

Is my thinking "all-or-nothing"? _____

_____

_____

Am I using emotional reasoning? _____

_____

_____

Am I minimizing the positive or maximizing the negative?

Am I using overgeneralizations?

Am I personalizing anything?

Analyzing Options:

Making Proposals:

MANAGED EMOTIONS

Emotion Check:

Did I remember to breathe?

Did I raise my voice?

Did I yell or scream?

_____
_____
_____

Did I threaten anything?

_____
_____
_____

Did I say regrettable things?

_____
_____
_____

Did I upset the other person?

_____
_____
_____

Did my anger get in the way of my message?

_____
_____
_____

Calming others with EAR (Empathy, Attention and/or Respect)

_____
_____
_____
_____
_____

Create some STARs (Statements That Are Reinforcing)

_____
_____

MODERATE BEHAVIOR

Behavior Check:

Did I insult anyone?

_____
_____
_____

Was I rude or inappropriate?

_____
_____
_____

Was my behavior aggressive?

_____
_____
_____

Did I go against any work policies? (Late, missed meetings, missed deadlines, absences, etc.)

_____
_____
_____

Did my behavior put myself or others at risk?

_____
_____
_____

Could I have substituted a moderate behavior?

_____
_____
_____

New behavior goal at work:

_____
_____
_____

Practicing new behaviors to get to the goal:

_____
_____
_____

CHECK YOURSELF – CHECKLIST

Situation: _____

_____

_____

Think Check:

Is my thinking "all-or-nothing"?

_____

_____

Am I using emotional reasoning?

_____

_____

Am I minimizing the positive or maximizing the negative?

_____

_____

Am I using overgeneralizations?

_____

_____

Am I personalizing anything?

_____

_____

Am I making any assumptions?

_____

_____

Emotion Check:

Did I remember to breathe?

_____

_____

Did I raise my voice or scream?

Did I threaten anything?

Did I say regrettable things?

Did I upset the other person?

Did my anger get in the way of my message?

Behavior Check:

Did I insult anyone?

Was I rude or inappropriate?

Was my behavior aggressive?

I did go against any work policies?   (Late, missed meetings, missed deadlines, absences, etc.)

Did my behavior put myself or others at risk?

Could I have substituted a moderate behavior?

CONCLUSION TO COACHING MANUAL

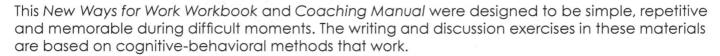

This *New Ways for Work Workbook* and *Coaching Manual* were designed to be simple, repetitive and memorable during difficult moments. The writing and discussion exercises in these materials are based on cognitive-behavioral methods that work.

Ideally, by doing all of the writing assignments in the Workbook, the client will improve deficient behavior and improve general work relationships in order to maintain or advance in his or her career.

This is a new approach and it is hoped that it will be used throughout an organization, so that the skills can be reinforced by management and co-workers for everyone's benefit before, during and after there have been difficulties for one or more individuals or groups.

MANAGEMENT REVIEW OF PROGRESS

After an employee who was referred by management for a behavior problem has gone through *New Ways for Work* Coaching, their behavior will hopefully have improved. A manager will notice if changes have been made in line with the skills taught in the Workbook, or not. If an employee is unable to perform adequately, even after going through this structured coaching process, it may mean that the employee is unlikely to change and may have a more fundamental resistance to change as part of who he or she is.

MEDIATION OF TWO OR MORE EMPLOYEES

Sometimes there has been a conflict between two or more employees and it is not clear who has acted badly, or if it is clear but there is hope for an improved relationship. Having a mediation of a dispute where there may be a power imbalance, such as bullying, may best occur after all parties involved have gone through this coaching process. Then, each party to the conflict may be more aware of how to work on changing his or her own behavior. Only when this type of self-reflection may be occurring would it be likely to have a positive mediation of some types of workplace disputes.

As always, the decisions of what to do in the future in the workplace are up to the individual and the organization.

Congratulations on completing this Coaching process and Best Wishes in the future!

APPENDIX

ARTICLES

(These articles do not appear in the Workbook, but may be copied and given to clients and distributed to colleagues, so long as they are not altered.)

Calming Upset People with EAR

Coaching for BIFF Responses

Calming Upset People with E.A.R.

By Bill Eddy, LCSW, Esq.

Everyone gets upset some of the time. High conflict people get upset a lot of the time. A simple technique called an "E.A.R. Statement" can help you calm others down. This is especially helpful if you are in a close relationship or a position of authority. High conflict people tend to emotionally attack those closest to them and those in authority when they are frustrated and can't manage their own emotions. The intensity of their uncontrolled emotions can really catch you off-guard. But if you practice making E.A.R. statements you can really connect with upset people, which is really what they want.

E.A.R. Statements

E.A.R. stands for Empathy, Attention and Respect. It is the opposite of what you feel like giving someone when he or she is upset and verbally attacking YOU! Yet you will be amazed at how effective this is when you do it right.

An E.A.R. Statement connects with the person's experience, with their feelings. For example, let's say that someone verbally attacks you for not returning a phone call as quickly as he or she would have liked. "You don't respect me! You don't care how long I have to wait to deal with this problem! You're not doing your job!"

Rather than defending yourself, give the person an E.A.R. Statement, such as: "Wow, I can hear how upset you are. Tell me what's going on. I share your concerns about this problem and respect your efforts to solve it." This statement included:

EMPATHY: "I can hear how upset you are."

ATTENTION: "Tell me what's going on."

RESPECT: "I respect your efforts."

The Importance of Empathy

Empathy is different from sympathy. Having empathy for someone means that you can feel the pain and frustration that they are feeling, and probably have felt similar feelings in your own life. These are normal human emotions and they are normally triggered in the people nearby. (Emotions are contagious!) When you show empathy for another person, you are treating them as a peer who you are concerned about and can relate to as an equal in distress.

Sympathy is when you see someone else in a bad situation that you are not in. You may feel sorry for them and have sympathy for them, but it is a one-up and one-down position. There is more of a separation between those who give sympathy and those who receive it.

You don't have to use the word "empathy" to make a statement that shows empathy. For example:

"I can see how important this is to you."
"I understand this can be frustrating."
"I know this process can be confusing."
"I'm sorry to see that you're in this situation."
"I'd like to help you if I can."
"Let's see if we can solve this together."

The Importance of Attention

There are many ways to let a person know that you will pay attention. For example, you can say:

"I will listen as carefully as I can."
"I will pay attention to your concerns."
"Tell me what's going on."
"Tell me more!"

You can also show attention non-verbally, such as:

Have good "eye contact" (keeping your eyes focused on the person)
Nod your head up and down to show that you are attentive to their concerns
Lean in to pay closer attention
Put your hand near them, such as on the table beside them
(but be careful about touching an upset HCP – it may be misinterpreted as a threat, a come-on, or a put-down)

The Importance of Respect

Anyone in distress, and especially HCPs, need respect from others. Even the most difficult and upset person usually has some quality that you can respect. By recognizing that quality, you can calm a person who is desperate to be respected. Here are several statements showing respect:

"I can see that you are a hard worker."
"I respect your commitment to solving this problem."
"I respect your efforts on this."
"I respect your success at accomplishing _____."
"You have important skills that we need here."

Why E.A.R. is so Important to HCPs

They're not getting it anywhere else. They have usually alienated most of the people around them. It is the last thing that anyone wants to give them. They are used to being rejected, abandoned, insulted, ignored, and disrespected by those around them. They are starving for empathy, attention and respect. They are looking for it anywhere they can get it. So just give it to them. It's free and you don't sacrifice anything. You can still set limits, give bad news, and keep a social or professional distance. It just means that you can connect with them around solving a particular problem and treat them like an equal human being, whether you agree or strongly disagree with their part in the problem.

What to Avoid

Don't Lie
You don't have to listen forever
E.A.R. doesn't mean you agree
Maintain an "arms-length" relationship

Manage Your Amygdala

Of course, this is the opposite of what we feel like doing. You may think to yourself: "No way I'm going to listen to this after how I've been verbally attacked!" But that's just your amygdala talking, in an effort to protect you from danger. Our brains are very sensitive to threats, especially our amygdalas (you have one in the middle of your right hemisphere and one in the middle of your left). Most people, while growing up, learn to manage the impulsive, protective responses of their amygdalas and over-ride them with a rational analysis of the situation, using their prefrontal context behind the forehead.

In fact, that is a lot of what adolescence is about: learning what is a crisis needing an instant, protective response (amygdale) and learning what situations are not a crisis and instead need a calm and rational response (prefrontal cortext). High conflict people often were abused or entitled growing up, and didn't have the secure, balanced connection necessary to learn these skills of emotional self-management. Therefore, you can help them by helping yourself not over-react to them – use your own prefrontal cortext to manage your amygdala.

It's Not About You!

Remind yourself it's not about you! Don't take it personally. It's about the person's own upset and lack of sufficient skills to manage his or her own emotions. Try making E.A.R. statements and you will find they often end the attack and calm the person down. This is especially true for high conflict people (HCPs) who regularly have a hard time calming themselves down.

All of these are calming statements. They let the person know that you want to connect with him or her, rather than threaten him or her.

Conclusion

Making E.A.R. statements – or non-verbally showing your Empathy, Attention and Respect – may help you avoid many potentially high-conflict situations. It can save you time, money and emotional energy for years to come.

High Conflict Institute provides training, books and consultations regarding High Conflict People (HCPs) for professionals dealing with legal, workplace, healthcare and educational disputes. Bill Eddy is the President of High Conflict Institute and the author of "*It's All YOUR Fault! 12 Tips for Managing People Who Blame Others for Everything.*" He is an attorney, mediator and therapist. Bill has presented seminars to attorneys, judges, mediators, ombudspersons, human resource professionals, employee assistance professionals, managers and administrators in over 25 states, several provinces in Canada, France and Australia. For more information about High Conflict Institute, our seminars or consultations, or Bill Eddy and his books, go to: www.HighConflictInstitute.com or call 619-221-9108.

Coaching for
BIFF Responses

By Bill Eddy, LCSW, Esq.

BIFF responses are designed to calm a hostile conversation. They can be written (or said) by anyone. However, it takes practice and helps to have someone review your BIFF response before you send it. BIFF stands for Brief, Informative, Friendly and Firm. This method is described in depth in the book *BIFF: Quick Responses to High Conflict People, Their Personal Attacks, Hostile Email and Social Media Meltdowns.*

Many people today are Coaches who are trained to assist individuals who are working on improving their interpersonal skills and/or dealing with a high conflict situation. This article is designed for professionals serving as Coaches, but it can be applied by anyone helping anyone write an effective BIFF Response.

Since High Conflict Institute was established four years ago, we have coached business partners, human resource professionals, neighbors, parents of adult children, spouses going through a divorce, and many others. We have learned that coaching for BIFF responses can be highly effective if the Coach asks the following ten questions of the individual who has written a draft of a BIFF Response (who I'll call the "Client" – whether it's a business client, friend or family member).

1. Is it Brief?

2. Is it Informative?

3. Is it Friendly?

4. Is it Firm?

5. Does it contain any Advice?

6. Does it contain any Admonishments?

7. Does it contain any Apologies?

8. How do you think the other person will respond?

9. Is there anything you would take out, add or change?

10. Would you like to hear my thoughts about it?

The Goal of Coaching for a BIFF Response

To be most helpful, a Coach for a BIFF response should point out that there is no single "right" way to write a BIFF response. In many ways it's like cooking. What works for one person is almost always different from what works for another person. The BIFF response always belongs to the person writing it. It is very important for the BIFF Coach to avoid "correcting" the Client's BIFF response as soon as it has been written. The goal is to help the Client *learn to write* BIFF responses, so he or she can do them on their own in the future, if necessary. The only way to effectively do that is to help the Client *analyze his or her own* BIFF response. These questions keep the focus on helping the Client do just that.

You will notice that the last question is *"Would you like to hear my thoughts about it?"* You might wonder why that isn't the first question. You might really, really want to give suggestions right away. But by keeping this question for last, you put the focus on having the client really think about what he or she has written. This means that when you ask the first question, *"Is it Brief?"* you are careful not to start suggesting how it could be longer or shorter. Let the person think about it for a moment and decide for him or herself.

It helps to introduce these ten questions with an explanation like this:

> "Whenever we write a BIFF response, it helps to discuss it with someone else before we send it. When I've given my BIFF drafts to someone else, they have usually suggested that I trim them down – sometimes even cutting them in half! And I've usually agreed! It's hard to see in our own comments what might trigger more anger or misbehavior from the other person. It's often easier for someone else to spot those trigger words or sentences. But I want to start out by letting you analyze your BIFF response, as this will help you get better and better at writing BIFFs that accomplish what you want.

> "So I would like you to read your BIFF out loud. Then, I'm going to help you by asking you 10 questions, so you can think about your BIFF. And remember, there's no one right way of writing a BIFF. My goal is to help you think about whether it will accomplish what *you* want with the person *you* are dealing with at this time."

BIFF Writers Feel Vulnerable

One thing we have learned about coaching BIFF clients is that they often feel very vulnerable, because they are usually dealing with a high conflict person (an HCP) who is criticizing them mercilessly or making the Client's life miserable in some other way. When they write a BIFF response, they are trying to regain a sense of balance and peace, so it is a time when they are very vulnerable to the feedback of others. Therefore, it is very important that they feel safe with you, rather than even a hint of personal criticism, as you help them decide whether they believe it's going to be an effective BIFF.

With this in mind, it helps to be supportive and encouraging during the first nine questions, rather than exact. Your response to their answers can be positive, while leaving room for you to make suggestions at the end with question #10. So when your Client says: "I think it's Brief," you can say "It looks like that to me too" and move on. Then, when you get to say your thoughts at the end (but only if the person says "Yes, I want to hear your thoughts"), you can say something like this: "While it looks Brief, you might want to take out the third sentence, and make it even briefer. That sentence seems like it might trigger an emotional response because of … But of course, it's up to you. It's your BIFF. What do you think about that?"

You can use a similar response when the person thinks about whether it's Informative. This questioning process does not need a big response. Most often the person will simply say: "Yes, I think its Informative." Then you can say: "Ok. And do you think that it's Friendly?" You can go through this questioning process quickly or slowly, depending on what the Client wants to say about it.

Sometimes, the Client will spontaneously decide to change something. That's great! In this situation, you can ask the Client what he or she thinks about it now. You might ask your Client to read it out loud again and see what they think. Remember to keep the focus on *the Client's analysis* of the BIFF – not yours.

The Triple A's

The Triple A's are: Advice, Admonishments and Apologies. These are less obvious than the first four questions about a BIFF response and are a whole chapter in the BIFF book. If your Client is not familiar with the Triple A's or has forgotten them, you can briefly explain these when you ask questions 5-7:

> "5.   Does it contain any Advice? By this, I mean are you telling the other person how to deal with a particular problem a particular way? This almost always triggers a defensive and often attacking response back at you. Unless the person you're dealing with specifically asked for your advice, it's usually better not to give it – especially in a BIFF response that's intended to end the conversation or give two limited choices. So do you see any advice in your BIFF as its currently written?"

> "6.   Does it contain any Admonishments? In other words, are you speaking to the person like a parent telling a child how to behave. This never works in a BIFF. When people are feeling defensive, the last thing they want is for you to tell them they are doing something wrong. The whole point of a BIFF is to calm down and end the conversation, without triggering a defensive response. Do you see any hint of that in your BIFF as it is currently written?"

> "7.   Does it contain any Apologies? This can be confusing. In general, apologies are a good thing. However, if you are dealing with a high conflict person, they tend to use your apologies against you, like ammunition. Avoid apologizing for anything of substance, like: "I shouldn't have done such-and-such." Or: "I'm sorry I hurt you by doing xyz." Or: "I guess my strategy failed." Or: "I know I haven't been sensitive to your needs." These types of apologizes blame you and HCPs are preoccupied with blame, and will use it to prove that it really is: All YOUR Fault! Of course, social apologies are okay, like "I'm sorry I'm a few minutes late." Or: "I'm sorry to see that you're in this difficult situation." With this in mind, do you see any apologies in what you have written?"

Your Thoughts

When you finally get to your thoughts – if you have been asked to give them – it is important to make them tentative. Remember, there's no one right answer and it's up to the Client to decide how it is written. For example, "You might want to think about that third sentence. I think it *might* trigger an intense response from the person you're dealing with, because he or she already said such-and-such. What do you think?"

Suppose the Client says: "I agree it should be changed. How should I say it?" Ideally, you will respond by saying: "Why don't you give it a try first, and see how it sounds. You've been doing great so far." This keeps the emphasis on your goal, which is to help the Client do his or her *own analysis* of the BIFF. It also helps boost the Client's confidence, at a time when he or she may be feeling extremely vulnerable about writing anything, because of so much criticism from the person they're dealing with.

If you decide to give a suggestion, try to give two or three: "You might try saying '…" or you might try saying it this other way "…." What do you think?" This helps them continue to think about it and make it their own writing, rather than simply doing what you said. The best coaching is when the Client feels smart, rather feeling that the Coach is brilliant. When you're coaching, it's not about you.

An Example

Suppose your client, Sam, has written the following BIFF response draft and ready to discuss it:

> "Yolanda, thank you for your email. I thought about it a lot. I agree we should stop doing our math homework together. It will help us each try harder to learn it ourselves. But I disagree that I was just "using" you and not helping you at all. I'm still glad that we're friends and will talk about other things when we're together. Sam."

After you've gone through all your questions, Sam asks you for your thoughts. It could go like this:

> Coach: "Overall, I really like it. However, I'm concerned that the phrase 'using you' might backfire. Yolanda might focus on that and attack you back, such as: 'Well, you WERE using me. I'M the one who figured out how to really do the assignment.' Then, Sam, you'll feel even more defensive. What do you think about leaving out that phrase? Or even that whole sentence?"

> Sam: "But I can't just let her think I was using her, because I wasn't!"

> Coach: "Well, it's up to you, of course. But from what you've told me, I don't think you will prove anything to her on this subject. If YOU are confident that you weren't using her, then do you really need to even discuss it with her? Especially in this BIFF? Perhaps you could tell just her that sometime when you are being friends talking about something else."

> Sam: "I'll have to think about it."

> Coach: "Why don't you try reading it without that third sentence, and then decide."

> Sam: " 'Yolanda, thank you for your email. I thought about it a lot. I agree we should stop doing our math homework together. It will help us each try harder to learn it ourselves. I'm still glad that we're friends and will talk about other things when we're together.'"

> Sam: "You're right. It does sound better that way."

> Coach: "Great! Let me know how it works out after you send it."

And then you can tell yourself (privately): "Way to go, Coach!"

Bill Eddy is the author of several books, including *BIFF: Quick Responses to High Conflict People, Their Personal Attacks, Hostile Email and Social Media Meltdowns* and the President of the High Conflict Institute. High Conflict Institute offers seminars, consultations (including BIFF Consultations), books and other resources for dealing with difficult people at work, at school, in divorce and anywhere. For more information: www.HighConflictInstitute.com or 619-221-9108.